Student Book

M000265893

2

ignite
English

Christopher Edge

Liz Hanton

Mel Peeling

Martin Phillips

Alison Smith

Consultant

Geoff Barton

OXFORD
UNIVERSITY PRESS

OXFORD
UNIVERSITY PRESS

Great Clarendon Street, Oxford, OX2 6DP, United Kingdom

Oxford University Press is a department of the University of Oxford. It furthers the University's objective of excellence in research, scholarship, and education by publishing worldwide. Oxford is a registered trade mark of Oxford University Press in the UK and in certain other countries

© Oxford University Press 2014

First published in 2014

All rights reserved. No part of this publication may be reproduced, stored in a retrieval system, or transmitted, in any form or by any means, without the prior permission in writing of Oxford University Press, or as expressly permitted by law, by licence or under terms agreed with the appropriate reprographics rights organization. Enquiries concerning reproduction outside the scope of the above should be sent to the Rights Department, Oxford University Press, at the address above.

You must not circulate this work in any other form and you must impose this same condition on any acquirer

British Library Cataloguing in Publication Data

Data available

978-0-19-839243-9

11

Paper used in the production of this book is a natural, recyclable product made from wood grown in sustainable forests. The manufacturing process conforms to the environmental regulations of the country of origin.

Printed and bound by CPI Group (UK) Ltd, Croydon, CR0 4YY

Acknowledgements

The authors and publisher would like to thank the following for permissions to use their photographs:

Cover: Janaka Dharmasena/Shutterstock; wolfmaster13/Shutterstock: Ecelop/Shutterstock; Serg64/Shutterstock; mhatzapa/Shutterstock; agrino/Shutterstock; IanC66/Shutterstock; SOTK2011/Alamy; **p8-9:** siloto/Shutterstock; **p8:** Morphart Creation/Shutterstock; **p10-11:** Seamartini Graphics/Shutterstock; **p11:** maximimages.com/Alamy; **p12-13:** vvoe/Shutterstock; **p14:** eye35/Alamy; **p14:** jossnat/Shutterstock; **p16-17:** conrado/Shutterstock; **p16:** Brocorwin/Shutterstock; **p18:** Everett Collection/Shutterstock; **p19:** Feng Yu/Shutterstock; **p19:** YVES HERMAN/ Reuters/Corbis; **p20-21:** kilukilu/Shutterstock; **p21:** jgl247/Shutterstock; **p22-23:** Lordprice Collection/Alamy; **p22:** ostill/Shutterstock; **p23:** Photos 12/Alamy; **p23:** AF archive / Alamy; **p24-25:** Denis Barbulat/Shutterstock; **p25:** Patricia Hofmeester/Shutterstock; **p27:** momanuma/Shutterstock; **p28:** siloto/Shutterstock; **p29:** Diane Diederich/ Getty Images (RF); **p29:** Grant Glendinning/Shutterstock; **p29:** ID1974/Shutterstock.com; **p29:** Johanna Nyholm/ Johnér Images/Corbis; **p29:** liseykina/Shutterstock; **p29:** SUSAN LEGGETT/Shutterstock; **p29:** Texturis/Shutterstock; **p30-31:** Andrey_Kuzmin/Shutterstock; **p30:** Lorelyn Medina/Shutterstock; **p30:** Undergroundarts.co.uk/ Shutterstock; **p32-33:** IWM via Getty Images; **p32-33:** IWM via Getty Images; **p32-33:** n_fransua/Shutterstock; **p32:** Mary Evans/Robert Hunt Collection; **p33:** Hulton Archive/Getty Images; **p34-35:** Marko Marcello/Shutterstock; **p34:** Liddle Museum Objects AW115/Digital Library Leeds; **p34:** Pictorial Press Ltd/Alamy; **p34:** Stapleton Collection/ Corbis; **p35:** Karina Bakalyan/Shutterstock; **p35:** Susan Law Cain/Shutterstock.com; **p36-37:** Hulton Archive/Getty Images; **p36:** The Art Archive/Alamy; **p38-39:** Classic Image/Alamy; **p38-39:** Silhouette Lover/Shutterstock; **p38:** Imperial War Museum; **p39:** cosma/Shutterstock; **p39:** Everett Collection/Shutterstock; **p39:** Pakhnyushcha/ Shutterstock; **p39:** zimand/Shutterstock; **p40-41:** Chrislofotos/Shutterstock; **p40:** 501room/Shutterstock; **p40:** Pictorial Press Ltd/Alamy; **p42-43:** Annavee/Shutterstock; **p42:** Hulton Archive/Getty Images; **p42:** National Library of Scotland; **p43:** Robert Hunt Library/Mary Evans; **p44-45:** Santiago Cornejo/Shutterstock; **p44:** Imperial War Museum/The Bridgeman Art Library; **p45:** DEA/E. LESSING/Getty Images; **p46-47:** The Art Gallery Collection/Alamy; **p46-47:** The Art Gallery Collection/Alamy; **p48-49:** Bettmann/CORBIS; **p48:** Bettmann/CORBIS; **p48:** Doug Steley B/ Alamy; **p48:** Hulton Archive/Getty Images; **p49:** oliver leedham/Alamy; **p50-51:** Imperial War Museum; **p51:** Corbis; **p52-53:** Peshkova/Shutterstock; **p54:** US ARMY/SCIENCE PHOTO LIBRARY; **p55:** PCN Photography/Alamy; **p60-61:** Valentin Agapov/Shutterstock; **p60:** Hein Nouwens/Shutterstock; **p61:** Mary Evans Picture Library/Alamy; **p62-63:** Gwoeii/Shutterstock; **p62:** matka_Wariatka/Shutterstock; **p65:** SeDmi/Shutterstock; **p66-67:** Antonio Abrignani/ Shutterstock; **p66-67:** Antonio Abrignani/Shutterstock; **p66-67:** Walker Art Library/Alamy; **p68-69:** Piotr Krzeslak/ Shutterstock; **p68:** Hintau Aliaksei/Shutterstock; **p68:** Sashkin/Shutterstock; **p69:** Potapov Alexander/Shutterstock; **p70-71:** dibrova/Shutterstock; **p70-71:** taviphoto/Shutterstock; **p70:** Boykung/Shutterstock; **p72-73:** Anneka/ Shutterstock; **p73:** AF archive/Alamy; **p73:** Lonely/Shutterstock; **p74-75:** Thumbelina/Shutterstock; **p74-75:** Thumbelina/Shutterstock; **p74:** Elnur/Shutterstock; **p74:** Stephen Coburn/Shutterstock; **p75:** Elnur/Shutterstock; **p75:** TerraceStudio/Shutterstock; **p76:** Lebrecht Music and Arts Photo Library/Alamy; **p76:** Steve Collender/ Shutterstock; **p77:** Andrew Burgess/Shutterstock; **p77:** Chris Hellier/ Alamy; **p78-79:** tratong/Shutterstock; **p78:** elic/Shutterstock; **p78:** MetCreations/Shutterstock; **p78:** MidoSemsem/Shutterstock; **p78:** S1001/Shutterstock; **p78:** vilax/Shutterstock; **p79:** Coprid/Shutterstock; **p79:** Irmairma/Shutterstock; **p79:** Margo Harrison/Shutterstock; **p79:** NinaMalyna/Shutterstock; **p80:** borkiss/Shutterstock; **p80:** Craig Wactor/Shutterstock; **p80:** gresei/Shutterstock; **p80:** igor.stevanovic/Shutterstock; **p80:** Sarah Marchant/Shutterstock; **p80:** Tarzhanova/Shutterstock; **p81:** Africa Studio/Shutterstock; **p81:** Africa Studio/Shutterstock; **p81:** Designsstock/Shutterstock; **p81:** imagehub/Shutterstock; **p81:** mayakova/Shutterstock; **p81:** Petr Malyshev/Shutterstock; **p81:** Ruslan Kudrin/Shutterstock; **p82-83:** Bad Man Production/Shutterstock; **p82:** Creativa/Shutterstock; **p82:** Hein Nouwens/Shutterstock; **p82:** Sergey Nivens/ Shutterstock; **p83:** avarand/Shutterstock; **p84:** James Steidl/Shutterstock; **p84:** North Wind Picture Archives/ Alamy; **p85:** The Art Archive/Alamy; **p86-87:** Fedor A. Sidorov/Shutterstock; **p86-87:** Maslov Dmitry/Shutterstock; **p86-87:** mirrormere/Shutterstock; **p86-87:** Wuttichok Painichiwarapu/Shutterstock; **p88-89:** Studiojumpee/Shutterstock; **p88:** calvindexter/Shutterstock; **p89:** Keystone Pictures USA/Alamy; **p90-91:** Adlens Ltd. All rights reserved. John Lennon™ graphic based on the original photo by Iain MacMillan 1971. Eagle Eyewear, Inc. Is the exclusive creator and master eyewear licensee of The John Lennon™ Eyewear Collection. ©Yoko Ono Lennon. Licensed exclusively by Bag One Arts. Lennon™ and John Lennon™ are Trademarks of Yoko Ono Lennon.; **p92-93:** SkillUp/Shutterstock; **p94-95:** US Coast Guard Photo/Alamy; **p96-97:** nito/Shutterstock; **p96:** ZUMA Press, Inc./Alamy; **p96:** ZUMA Press, Inc./Alamy; **p97:** ZUMA Press, Inc. /Alamy; **p98-99:** Green Jo/Shutterstock; **p98-99:** gualtiero boffi/Shutterstock; **p98-99:** Maxx-Studio/Shutterstock; **p98-99:** yuyangc/Shutterstock; **p99:** RTimages/Shutterstock; **p100-101:** Mopic/ Shutterstock; **p100-101:** PremiumVector/Shutterstock; **p100:** dream designs/Shutterstock; **p100:** Kokhanchikov/ Shutterstock; **p101:** siraphat/Shutterstock; **p101:** Stocksolutions/Alamy; **p101:** Vankad/Shutterstock; **p102:** Elena Schweitzer/Shutterstock; **p102:** Konstantin Sutyagin/Shutterstock; **p103:** saknakorn/Shutterstock; **p103:** samarttiw/Shutterstock; **p103:** Silhouette Lover/Shutterstock; **p104-105:** SergeyIT/Shutterstock; **p104:** Eric Milos/ Shutterstock; **p104:** Hill120/Shutterstock; **p104:** Igor Karasi/Shutterstock; **p104:** Potapov Alexander/Shutterstock; **p105:** Petr Student/Shutterstock; **p106-107:** Conrad Elias/Alamy; **p106-107:** irin-k/Shutterstock; **p106:** paintings/ Shutterstock; **p107:** Dariush M/Shutterstock; **p107:** Glynnis Jones/Shutterstock; **p107:** Peshkova/Shutterstock; **p107:** VoodooDot/Shutterstock; **p107:** waniuszka/Shutterstock; **p108-109:** British Heart Foundation; **p108-109:** British Red Cross; **p108-109:** Children in Need; **p108-109:** Napat/Shutterstock; **p108-109:** Oxfam; **p108-109:** World Wildlife Fund; **p108:** Asaf Eliason/Shutterstock; **p108:** Asaf Eliason/Shutterstock; **p108:** Photocuisine/Alamy; **p108:** REX/Sipa USA; **p108:** tristan tan/Shutterstock; **p108:** vadimmmus/Shutterstock; **p110:** Feng Yu/Shutterstock; **p110:** Ian Dagnall/Alamy; **p110:** redsnapper/Alamy; **p111:** Asaf Eliason/Shutterstock; **p111:** Martin Cameron/ Alamy; **p111:** testing/Shutterstock; **p112:** Dr. Morley Read/Shutterstock; **p112:** lculig/Shutterstock; **p112:** Ocskay Bence/Shutterstock; **p114-115:** Caro/Alamy; **p114:** Dan Kosmayer/Shutterstock; **p114:** epa european pressphoto agency b.v./Alamy; **p114:** theodore liasi/ Alamy; **p116-117:** Jktu_21/Shutterstock; **p116-117:** Roman Sotola/ Shutterstock; **p116:** Julia Ivantsova/Shutterstock; **p117:** Butterfly Hunter/Shutterstock; **p117:** Maxx-Studio/ Shutterstock; **p117:** rvlsoft/Shutterstock; **p118:** SAM OGDEN/SCIENCE PHOTO LIBRARY; **p119:** Mega Pixel/ Shutterstock; **p120-121:** Melanie Blanding/Alamy; **p121:** George Osodi/Panos; **p122-123:** Evgeny Karandaev/ Shutterstock; **p122-123:** Oleksiy Mark/Shutterstock; **p122-123:** Reinhold Leitner/Shutterstock; **p124-125:** Aaron Amat/Shutterstock; **p124-125:** FLPA/Alamy; **p124:** Carolyn Jenkins/Alamy; **p125:** Andris Tkacenko/Shutterstock; **p125:** EIGHTFISH/Alamy; **p126:** betty finney/Alamy; **p128-129:** Philip Lange/Shutterstock; **p128:** L F File/ Shutterstock; **p129:** epa european pressphoto agency b.v./Alamy; **p130-131:** epa european pressphoto agency b.v./ Alamy; **p130:** xiver/Shutterstock; **p134-135:** Binkski/Shutterstock; **p134:** Andrey Eremin/Shutterstock; **p134:** War Archive/Alamy; **p138-139:** concept w/Shutterstock; **p138:** Blackberry Trafficmaster; **p139:** SAMSUNG ELECTRONICS CO. LTD; **p141:** The LEGO Group; **p141:** Hasbro Ltd; **p143:** Dogs Trust; **p143:** Eric Isselee/Shutterstock; **p144-145:** hxdbzxy/Shutterstock; **p145:** Ilya D. Gridnev/Shutterstock; **p146-147:** Alex Segre/Alamy; **p147:** greenland/ Shutterstock; **p148-149:** rangizzz/Shutterstock; **p148:** Oleksiy Maksymenko Photography/Alamy; **p149:** Matusciac Alexandru/Shutterstock, InnervisionArt/Shutterstock; p149: Matusciac Alexandru/Shutterstock; **p150-151:** LanaN/ Shutterstock; **p151:** David Cole / Alamy; **p151:** Keystone Pictures USA/Alamy; **p151:** RetroClipArt/Shutterstock; **p152-153:** Nevena Radonja/Shutterstock; **p153:** Roman Gorielov/Shutterstock; **p154-155:** Everett Collection/ Shutterstock; **p156-157:** Pete Saloutos/Shutterstock; **p157:** SergeBertasiusPhotography/Shutterstock

All other images by New Future Graphic.

The authors and publisher are grateful for permission to reprint extracts from the following copyright material:

Simon Armitage: 'Out of the Blue' from *Out of the Blue* (Enitharmon 2008), copyright © Simon Armitage 2008, reprinted by permission of the publishers.

Stephanie Bannister: 'Women in cocoa production: Where is the gender equity?', theguardian.com, 8.3.2013, copyright © Guardian News and Media Ltd 2013, reprinted by permission of GNM Ltd.

K K Beck: 'Detective Stories' in *The Ultimate Teen Book Guide* edited by Daniel Hahn and Leonie Flynn (A & C Black, 2006), copyright © K K Beck 2006, reprinted by permission of the publishers, an imprint of Bloomsbury Publishing Plc.

John Boyne: *The Boy in Striped Pyjamas* (David Fickling, 2006), reprinted by permission of The Random House Group Ltd.

Raymond Chandler: *The Big Sleep* (Penguin 2011), copyright © Raymond Chandler 1939, reprinted by permission of Penguin Books

Angelique Chrisafis: 'Cannes jewellery heist takes shine off stars red carpet day', *The Guardian*, 17.5.2013, copyright © Guardian News and Media Ltd 2013, reprinted by permission of GNM Ltd.

Winston Churchill: 'Wars are not won by evacuations' speech given in the House of Commons, 4 June 1940, copyright © Winston S Churchill, reprinted by permission of Curtis Brown, London on behalf of the Estate of Sir Winston Churchill.

Siobhan Dowd: *The London Eye Mystery* (David Fickling Books, 2007), reprinted by permission of The Random House Group Ltd.

T S Eliot: lines from 'The Love Song of Alfred J Prufrock' from *Selected Poems of T S Eliot* (Faber, 2009), reprinted by permission of Faber & Faber Ltd.

Anne Fine: *Madame Doubtfire* (Penguin, 1998), copyright © Anne Fine 1987, reprinted by permission of Penguin Books Ltd and David Higham Associates.

Nadia Gilani: 'Big Brother Spyware Riot can even predict future crime', *Metro*, 11.2.2013, reprinted by permission of Solo Syndication.

Jonathan Kent: letter published in *The Daily Telegraph*, 11.4.2013, copyright © Telegraph Media Group 2013, reprinted by permission of TMG.

Denise Levertov: 'What Were they Like' from *New Selected Poems* (Bloodaxe, 2003), reprinted by permission of Bloodaxe Books

Thomas Frederick Littler: *Diary, June 7 1916*, published at www.first-world-war.co.uk/thediary, reprinted by permission of Chris Littler.

Erin Morgenstern: *The Night Circus: A Novel* (Harvill Secker, 2011), reprinted by permission of The Random House Group Ltd.

George Orwell: *Animal Farm* (Penguin Classics, 2000), copyright © George Orwell 1945, reprinted by permission of Bill Hamilton as the Literary Executor of the Estate of the late Sonia Brownell Orwell, c/o A M Heath & Co Ltd.

Wilfred Owen: letter to his mother Susan Owen from *Collected Letters edited by Harold Owen* (OUP, 1967), reprinted by permission of Oxford University Press.

Richard Platt: *Kingfisher Knowledge: Forensics* (Kingfisher, 2005), reprinted by permission of the publishers, an imprint of Macmillan Children's Books, London, UK.

Philip Pullman: *The Ruby in the Smoke* (Scholastic Children's Books, 1999, 2006), copyright © Philip Pullman 1985, reprinted by permission of Scholastic Ltd. All rights reserved.

Matilda Reid: 'Get Real. Banning adverts will not stop children wanting things', *The Daily Telegraph*, 11.4.2013, copyright © Telegraph Media Group 2013, reprinted by permission of TMG.

Siegfried Sassoon: 'Memorial Tablet', and 'Base Details' from *Collected Poems* (Faber, 2002); lines from 'Together' from *Counter Attack and Other Poems* (Heinemann, 1918); and *Siegfried Sassoon Diaries 1915-1918* edited by Rupert Hart-Davis (Faber, 1983), copyright © Siegfried Sassoon, reprinted by permission of the Estate of George Sassoon, c/o Barbara Levy Literary Agency.

Cameron Stewart (ed): *A Very Unimportant Officer: The Letters and Diaries of a Soldier on the Somme, 1916-1917* (Hodder & Stoughton, 2008) copyright © Diary and Letters, Alexander Stewart 1915, 1916, 1917, and 1928, reprinted by permission of Hodder & Stoughton Ltd.

Donna Tartt: *The Secret History* (Penguin, 2006/Viking 1992), copyright © Donna Tartt 1992, reprinted by permission of Penguin Books Ltd and Alfred A Knopf, an imprint of the Knopf Doubleday Publishing Group, a division of Random House LLC. All rights reserved.

and to the following for their permission to reprint extracts from copyright material:

BP for 'How we responded' from BP statement on 'Deepwater Horizon accident and response'.

Cornwall and Devon Media for 'Redruth's pioneering curfew slashes crime and anti-social behaviour' from West Briton, www.thisiscornwall.co.uk.

Dogs Trust, www.dogstrust.org.uk, for appeal letter, September 2012.

Oxfam America for extract from Oxfam Press Release, 8 March 2013, www.oxfam.org

Oxfam GB, Oxfam House, John Smith Drive, Cowley, Oxford, OX4 2JY, UK, for extract adapted from an Oxfam Case Study: Interview with James, Liberia, 20 May 2003, extract from *Oxfam Fact File on Liberia, Water Week Resources 2013*, from www.oxfam.org.uk/education; and Oxfam's template for possible press release from www.oxfam.org.uk. Oxfam GB does not necessarily endorse any text or activities that accompany the materials.

Although we have made every effort to trace and contact all copyright holders before publication this has not been possible in all cases. If notified, the publisher will rectify any errors or omissions at the earliest opportunity.

Links to third party websites are provided by Oxford in good faith and for information only. Oxford disclaims any responsibility for the materials contained in any third party website referenced in this work.

Ignite English has been written by people who love teaching English. It was a pre-requisite for us when developing this resource that you have people who are confident teaching English and who would find it patronizing to tell you how to teach English. Therefore we have provided a flexibility, both digitally and on the page, so that you can decide how you are going to customize it for your students.

In *Ignite English*, we also take English and show how it relates to the real world. Outside school there are lots of people doing lots of different jobs who will be using speaking, listening, reading and writing and we might not even think about how they are doing it. Well let's! In *Ignite English*, we take a look at what they do and we talk to them about how they are doing it, so that you and your students can explore the way they are using language and connect what we are doing in the classroom with the world out there.

Informed by research and recent Ofsted reports, *Ignite English* aims to help reinvigorate KS3 English teaching and learning by:

- Improving learning through relevance and creativity

- Ensuring teaching is distinctive

- Enabling effective transition between Year 6 and Year 7

- Accessing up-to-date and relevant professional development

- Delivering the new KS3 National Curriculum

That is essentially what we are trying to do with *Ignite English*.

Geoff Barton

Series Consultant, Head Teacher, Teacher of English and highly experienced English author

Ignite English authors

Ignite English was created with Geoff Barton and authored by experienced teachers and educationalists who are passionate about teaching English. As well as being tested in schools and reviewed by teachers, the resources were also reviewed by Peter Ellison, a cross-phase Local Authority Adviser and Phil Jarrett, former Ofsted National Adviser for English.

Contents

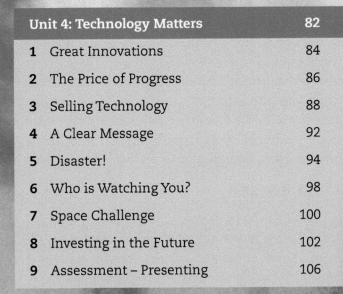

Overview of Ignite English

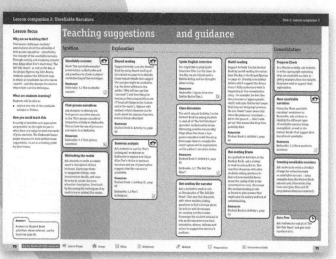

Transition support

Teacher Companion 1 includes English lesson suggestions and guidance on effective transition from Primary to Secondary school. It also includes a range of teaching ideas for the first week of English lessons in Secondary schools, with an opening lesson included in Student Book 1. In addition, there is a professional development unit specifically on transition in Kerboodle: Lessons, Resources and Assessments.

Also on Kerboodle LRA 1 and on the Oxford University Press *Ignite English* webpage, you will find a unit of work, with transition tips, for Primary school teachers to use in the final term of Year 6. This unit, 'Making a Difference', has *Ignite English* principles at its heart and we hope that by passing this unit on to local Primary schools it will foster enhanced relationships between Secondary school English departments and colleagues in local Primary schools.

Student Books

The Student Books have been designed to develop a range of reading, writing and spoken English skills in real-life contexts. Each Student Book offers thematically-focused units, covering prose fiction, poetry, drama and non-fiction forms, as well as a focus on language and one unique immersive unit based around a real-world scenario. They also feature an explicit focus on spelling, punctuation and grammar (SPAG). There is a wide range of source texts and activities with Stretch and Support as well as regular Progress Checks and Extra Time features, which can be used either for extension or homework.

Teacher Companions

Each Teacher Companion shares the thinking and philosophy behind the resources with a focus on the 'why', 'what' and 'how' of each unit, lesson and assessment. Additionally, the Teacher Companions feature unit-by-unit teaching support materials with comprehensive teaching tips, links and further reading suggestions. Each lesson features a Lesson Companion that includes a range of teaching ideas, guidance and tips to enable you to customize your lessons. The Teacher Companion also includes guidance and suggestions on setting up and marking the end of unit assessments.

Kerboodle: Lessons, Resources and Assessment

Kerboodle is packed full of guided support and ideas for creating and running effective lessons. It's intuitive to use, customizable, and can be accessed online anytime and anywhere. *Ignite English Kerboodle LRA* includes:

- 18 exclusive interviews providing over 40 unique and compelling films, connecting the learning in KS3 English lessons to skills used in thematically-linked jobs

- eight specially-commissioned filmed units providing CPD for English departments on key areas of Key Stage 3 teaching and learning, including genuine lesson footage, interviews with Primary and Secondary school teachers and students, and comments and observations from Geoff Barton and Phil Jarrett

- materials to support the transition for students from Key Stage 2 to Key Stage 3

- grammar support for teachers and students through extensive technical accuracy interactives and a grammar reference guide

- a wealth of additional resources including: interactive activities, an editable alternative end-of-unit assessment for every Student Book unit, marking scales to help monitor progress, photos, editable presentations, editable worksheets (general, differentiation and peer/self-assessment) and weblinks

- Lesson Player, enabling teachers to deliver ready-made lessons or the freedom to customize plans to suit your classes' needs.

Kerboodle Online Student Books

All three student books are also available as Online Student Books. These can be accessed on a range of devices, such as tablets, and offer a bank of tools to enable students to personalize their book and view notes left by the teacher.

Kate Geary and Matthew Grainger, Oxfam:
'Simplify the message.'

1 IT'S A MYSTERY

What's the formula to create a best-selling mystery?

CRIME SCENE

Introduction

A locked room, a scream of terror and a bloodied corpse – these are some of the ingredients you might find at the heart of a mystery. From bookshop shelves to prime-time TV, stories of crime and detection are big business. But how do mysteries work and could you find the formula to create your own best-seller?

In this unit, you will explore stories about great detectives and baffling mysteries, and develop your skills as a reader to unlock their secrets. Learning from some of the masters of the genre, you will write your own mystery story to publish and sell online.

ignite INTERVIEW
Christopher Edge, Mystery writer

One of the key things when you write is to show your excitement for the story. You need the detective to solve the crime, to investigate the puzzle that has been set at the start of the story. You need clues for that detective to follow. You need suspects, people who might be responsible for the crime and you need a villain, somebody who can be a real match to the hero that you have written about. When you are setting your own mystery stories, looking around at the places that inspire you is a key thing, but you can actually set your story anywhere.

✎ Activities

1 Discuss any mystery stories you have watched or read, e.g. The Sally Lockhart Mysteries by Philip Pullman or The Roman Mysteries by Caroline Lawrence. What did you enjoy about these stories?

2 Create a list of the features you expect to find in a mystery story, e.g. a puzzling crime. Give examples from stories you have watched or read for each feature in your list.

RETURN TICKET
238
RETURN TICKET

CRIME SCENE

1 Why Read Mysteries?

↺ Objective

Consider why readers may be attracted to particular genres.

ACTION
PLOT
CRIME CORPSES DANGER CLUES
GANGSTERS GUNS JUSTICE
CRIMINALS DETECTIVE SLEUTH
JEOPARDY
ACTION-PACKED
VIOLENT
SUSPENSE

What makes mystery stories so popular? Read the essay by the author K. K. Beck on page 11 where she explains why she thinks people should read detective fiction. Then complete the activities below.

✎ Activities

1 Discuss the different reasons the writer gives for reading detective novels.

2 Identify the reasons you find most persuasive. Use these reasons to create slogans for a school library display encouraging readers to try detective fiction, e.g. *Try out your detective skills with these dangerous reads.*

↔ Stretch

Think of your own arguments for reading detective fiction.

3a Look at the word cloud above. This shows some of the key words used in the article to describe detective fiction.

Think about a genre of books you enjoy reading, e.g. mysteries, adventure or supernatural stories. Create a word cloud of the key words that describe this genre for you.

3b Write a short article for your school magazine encouraging students to read books in the genre you chose for Activity 3a. Try to present your reasons persuasively, using some of the key words from your word cloud.

Extract from 'Detective Stories' by K. K. Beck

There are many reasons to read detective novels. First of all, you are pretty much guaranteed that things will happen and the plot will move along. That's because, with very few exceptions, a crime has already been, or is about to be, committed and must be solved. So the characters cannot just sit around. They are forced into action, which makes for a plot-driven, engaging read. And, because the criminals are still at large, and presumably don't want to be caught, the detectives are often in **jeopardy** as they go about their work. This means that the reader can enjoy the suspense of knowing the characters are in danger.

There's also something very satisfying about seeing a crime solved, getting everything properly sorted out, and making sure the guilty are exposed and presumably punished. If only justice always prevailed in real life! Plus, the reader can detect along with the characters. In classic, old-school detective fiction, the clues are usually arranged hiding in plain sight. The author's goal in these kinds of books is to get the reader to say 'Of course! Why didn't I see that?!' Agatha Christie is famous for these sorts of stories. In *The Secret Adversary*, two friends recently returned to London from World War I start their own detective agency, trace a girl named Jane Finn, and foil a plot to take over the world. Agatha Christie was also, of course, the creator of the great **sleuths** Miss Marple and Hercule Poirot.

There are all kinds of detectives, from **amateurs** who accidentally stumble on to a crime to hardened private eyes and police detectives. Because detective stories often feature the same detective in multiple books, after a little dabbling in the field it's easy to find the ones you know you'll enjoy. One of the first and best amateur detectives is Sherlock Holmes. *A Study in Scarlet* is the first Holmes mystery, but you needn't start there. Try *The Hound of the Baskervilles* or any of the 56 short stories. There's a reason Holmes and his sidekick Dr Watson have lasted so long.

Detective novels can be hard-boiled – violent and action-packed tales of guns and gangsters. Think of Raymond Chandler's *The Big Sleep*. They can be soft-boiled – gentle stories of pale corpses found neatly on the hearthrug in the vicarage in a quiet village – like Dorothy L. Sayers' Lord Peter Wimsey books. Or anything in between.

📖 Glossary

jeopardy danger

sleuths detectives

amateurs people who do something as a hobby, rather than as a paid job

🕒 Extra Time

Read and review a mystery story of your choice.

② What Makes a Mystery?

↻ Objective

Identify the typical features of the mystery genre.

Mystery stories usually include some or all of the following features:

- a puzzling problem or crime
- a detective or investigator
- suspects and a villain
- a trail of clues
- a final **plot twist**.

Read the extract on page 13 and then complete the activities on the right. The extract is from the opening of 'The Adventure of the Speckled Band' where a mysterious woman arrives at 221B Baker Street to see Sherlock Holmes.

◆ Activities

1 What features of the mystery genre can you find in this extract?

2 What impression do you get from this extract about:
- Sherlock Holmes
- the mysterious woman?

3 Why do you think the woman has come to see Sherlock Holmes? Make a prediction about what you think the case will be about.

Use what you already know about the woman and your knowledge of mystery stories to help you make your prediction.

4 Role-play the meeting between Sherlock Holmes and the mysterious woman. Draw on details from the extract and your own predictions to continue the conversation.

Extract from 'The Adventure of the Speckled Band' by Arthur Conan Doyle

A lady dressed in black and heavily veiled, who had been sitting in the window, rose as we entered.

'Good-morning, madam,' said Holmes cheerily. 'My name is Sherlock Holmes... I am glad to see that Mrs. Hudson has had the good sense to light the fire. Pray draw up to it, and I shall order you a cup of hot coffee, for I observe that you are shivering.'

'It is not cold which makes me shiver,' said the woman in a low voice, changing her seat as requested.

'What, then?'

'It is fear, Mr. Holmes. It is terror.' She raised her veil as she spoke, and we could see that she was indeed in a **pitiable** state of **agitation**, her face all drawn and grey, with restless frightened eyes, like those of some hunted animal. Her features and figure were those of a woman of thirty, but her hair was shot with premature grey, and her expression was weary and **haggard**. Sherlock Holmes ran her over with one of his quick, **all-comprehensive** glances.

'You must not fear,' said he soothingly, bending forward and patting her forearm. 'We shall soon set matters right, I have no doubt. You have come in by train this morning, I see.'

'You know me, then?'

'No, but I observe the second half of a return ticket in the palm of your left glove. You must have started early, and yet you had a good drive in a **dog-cart**, along heavy roads, before you reached the station.'

The lady gave a violent start and stared in bewilderment at my companion.

'There is no mystery, my dear madam,' said he, smiling. 'The left arm of your jacket is spattered with mud in no less than seven places. The marks are perfectly fresh. There is no vehicle save a dog-cart which throws up mud in that way, and then only when you sit on the left-hand side of the driver.'

'Whatever your reasons may be, you are perfectly correct,' said she. 'I started from home before six, reached Leatherhead at twenty past, and came in by the first train to Waterloo. Sir, I can stand this strain no longer; I shall go mad if it continues. I have no one to turn to – none, save only one, who cares for me, and he, poor fellow, can be of little aid. I have heard of you, Mr. Holmes; I have heard of you from Mrs. Farintosh, whom you helped in the hour of her sore need. It was from her that I had your address. Oh, sir, do you not think that you could help me, too, and at least throw a little light through the dense darkness which surrounds me? At present it is out of my power to reward you for your services, but in a month or six weeks I shall be married, with the control of my own income, and then at least you shall not find me ungrateful.'

📖 Glossary

plot twist   an unexpected event such as the death of a suspect that sends the plot in a new direction

pitiable   deserving sympathy

agitation   upset

haggard   tired-looking

all-comprehensive   taking in every detail

dog-cart   a horse-drawn carriage

3 Reading Detective

↻ Objective

Use inference and deduction to explore layers of meaning.

You need to read like a detective to work out exactly what is happening in the stories and texts you read. Close reading can help you to explore the details in a story and give you clues so that you can make **inferences** and **deductions**. In the extract from 'The Adventure of the Speckled Band' on page 13, Sherlock Holmes looks closely at his visitor to identify clues and then makes deductions from these.

✎ Activities

1 Re-read the extract on page 13 to pick out more clues about Holmes's visitor. Discuss what you can infer from each detail that you find.

📖 Glossary

inference a conclusion which is based on evidence

deduction the process of drawing a conclusion based on a general principle

Clues

'I observe the second half of a return ticket in the palm of your left glove... The left arm of your jacket is spattered with mud in no less than seven places. The marks are perfectly fresh.'

Deductions

'You have come in by train this morning... and yet you had a good drive in a dog-cart, along heavy roads, before you reached the station... There is no vehicle save a dog-cart which throws up mud in that way, and then only when you sit on the left-hand side of the driver.'

going to a funeral

shy

'dressed in black and heavily veiled'

ugly

doesn't want to be recognized

ignite INTERVIEW

'We can put ourselves in the shoes of the detective and try to almost beat the author to work out who is behind these mysteries before they have actually given away all the clues.'

Christopher Edge

2 As a reading detective, you can draw together different details to build up a more **forensic** analysis of a character, by looking at how the character acts, what they say and how they are described.

The lady in black
- how she is described
- how she acts
- what she says

Look at the spider diagram at the top of the page. Which do you think is the most likely reason for the woman to be 'dressed in black and heavily veiled'? Can you find any other evidence in the text to support this?

3 Review the details you have identified. Looking at these together, would you change any of the inferences and deductions you have made?

4 Write a paragraph explaining what you have inferred about the lady in black. You should include quotations from the extract to support your inferences.

📖 Glossary

forensic   using scientific and other techniques to study evidence in detail, usually to solve a crime

🕐 Extra Time

Find out more about Sherlock Holmes and his creator Arthur Conan Doyle. Why do you think Sherlock Holmes stories have been (and continue to be) so popular?

4 A Sense of Mystery

↻ Objective

Explore how vocabulary and subordinate clauses can be used to create suspense.

A mystery needs suspense to keep readers turning the pages. Read the extract on this page from the Sherlock Holmes story 'The Adventure of the Speckled Band' to explore how Arthur Conan Doyle creates suspense for his readers. Then complete the activities on page 17.

Sherlock Holmes has been visited by a young woman named Helen Stoner. She and her twin sister Julia lived in a crumbling manor house with their stepfather, Dr Grimesby Roylott, who benefited from an income left by their dead mother, but only as long as the sisters lived with him and did not marry. In this extract, Helen Stoner tells Holmes about the terrible fate that befell her twin sister two years earlier.

📖 Glossary

impending about to happen

blanched turned white

fain an old-fashioned word meaning 'readily'

Extract from 'The Adventure of the Speckled Band'

'I could not sleep that night. A vague feeling of **impending** misfortune impressed me [...] It was a wild night. The wind was howling outside, and the rain was beating and splashing against the windows. Suddenly, amid all the hubbub of the gale, there burst forth the wild scream of a terrified woman. I knew that it was my sister's voice. I sprang from my bed, wrapped a shawl round me, and rushed into the corridor. As I opened my door I seemed to hear a low whistle, such as my sister described, and a few moments later a clanging sound, as if a mass of metal had fallen. As I ran down the passage, my sister's door was unlocked, and revolved slowly upon its hinges. I stared at it horror-stricken, not knowing what was about to issue from it. By the light of the corridor-lamp I saw my sister appear at the opening, her face **blanched** with terror, her hands groping for help, her whole figure swaying to and fro like that of a drunkard. I ran to her and threw my arms round her, but at that moment her knees seemed to give way and she fell to the ground. She writhed as one who is in terrible pain, and her limbs were dreadfully convulsed. At first I thought that she had not recognized me, but as I bent over her she suddenly shrieked out in a voice which I shall never forget, 'Oh, my God! Helen! It was the band! The speckled band!' There was something else which she would **fain** have said, and she stabbed with her finger into the air in the direction of the doctor's room, but a fresh convulsion seized her and choked her words. I rushed out, calling loudly for my stepfather [...] When he reached my sister's side she was unconscious, and though he poured brandy down her throat and sent for medical aid from the village, all efforts were in vain, for she slowly sank and died without having recovered her consciousness. Such was the dreadful end of my beloved sister.'

Activities

1 Look at the sentence below which describes the moment Helen sees her sister. The positioning of the **subordinate clauses** adds to the suspense as the details describing Helen's sister are gradually revealed.

SPAG

Phrase

Main Clause

By the light of the corridor-lamp I saw my sister appear at the opening, her face blanched with terror, her hands groping for help, her whole figure swaying to and fro like that of a drunkard.'

Subordinate Clauses

Rewrite the sentence above by changing the position of the **main clause** and subordinate clauses. How many different sentences can you create? Decide which sentences are most effective in building suspense.

2 Identify the words and phrases used to create a tense and unsettling atmosphere. Look at:

- the way the weather is described
- the words the narrator uses to describe Helen's thoughts and reactions
- how the death of Helen's sister is described.

3 In the story, Helen Stoner then reveals that she had to move into the chamber where her sister died. One night, she suddenly heard the low whistle which had been the herald of her sister's death. Write the next few paragraphs of the story, using the techniques you have explored to create suspense and tension.

☑ Progress Check

Compare your paragraphs with a partner's. Ask them to give you two ratings, on a scale of 1 to 5, with 5 being the highest, on your use of:

- vocabulary to create a tense and unsettling atmosphere
- sentence structures to create a sense of suspense.

SPAG

📖 Glossary

subordinate clause clause which is dependent upon a main clause and cannot stand alone as a complete sentence

main clause clause which contains a subject and verb and makes sense on its own

⑤ Real-life Mysteries

↻ Objective

Investigate how you can take inspiration from real-life events to create your own mystery story.

Authors of crime and detective stories have often been inspired by real-life mysteries, while criminals in the real world have also found fictional inspiration for their crimes.

Read the newspaper report on page 19 about a daring jewellery theft, and then complete the activities below.

✎ Activities

1 Which fictional scripts does the writer of the article compare this crime to? Why do you think the writer chose to make these comparisons?

2 Think about how you could use this newspaper report to inspire your own mystery story. Re-read the report and note down details you could include in your story.

3 Role-play interviews with the following people to find out more about the crime:

- the jewellery company employee whose room was broken into
- the Hollywood actress who was going to wear the jewellery
- a hotel employee who might have spotted the crime taking place
- the police commander investigating the crime
- the criminal or criminals behind the theft.

4 Using your notes from Activity 2, write the opening of a mystery story based on this crime. You could also include details from the newspaper report or your role-play to create a dramatic opening for your story.

📚 Support

Try to grab the reader's attention from the very first line. You could start with a description of the theft or the discovery of the missing jewels. Think about how the details you include will hook the reader's interest.

CANNES JEWELLERY HEIST TAKES SHINE OFF STARS ON RED CARPET DAY

It could have been the plot of a Hollywood blockbuster: a thief creeps into a Cannes hotel room after dark and effortlessly makes off with over $1m worth of jewels destined to be worn by stars on the red carpet of the film festival.

The massive jewellery theft in the early hours of Friday was quickly likened to a scene from Alfred Hitchcock's 1950s Riviera robbery thriller, *To Catch a Thief*, with Cary Grant and Grace Kelly, where a mysterious cat burglar snatches the jewels of the rich and famous on the Côte d'Azur. But stranger still was the fact that the robbery took place just as all flashbulbs and press packs were focusing on Thursday night's premiere of Sofia Coppola's new film *The Bling Ring*, based on the true story of a group of suburban Los Angeles teenagers who stole luxury goods, jewels and watches from the houses of the rich and famous out of a desire to possess their wardrobes and emulate their lifestyles.

A safe box containing more than £660,000 worth of jewellery by the exclusive Swiss jeweller and watchmaker Chopard was removed from the wall of a room at the Suite Novotel. The room was reserved for an employee of the firm, which has sponsored the festival for 16 years and leads the way in the fiercely competitive race to showcase precious stones on the throats of the most famous stars.

On Friday, police continued to interview the Chopard employee, reportedly an American, as well as hotel staff at the Suite Novotel, a grey, modern block situated near a police station and a 15-minute walk from the more luxurious hotels of the Croisette. They were also examining hotel surveillance cameras.

Commander Bernard Mascarelli, a judicial police spokesman in Nice, said he did not know the precise type of jewels taken or their exact value [...]

Despite fears for the poor bare collarbones of famous stars, robbed of their diamonds for the weekend's premieres, the Cannes film festival continued uninterrupted on Friday.

6 Plotting the Perfect Crime

↻ Objective

Explore how to structure a mystery story.

A mystery story typically begins with a dramatic event, such as a description of a crime or the discovery of a body. The main character then discovers and follows clues, using these to track down suspects, before the mystery is solved at the story's climax. Mystery stories also include plot twists and **red herrings** to surprise the reader and build tension in the story.

Look at the graph below, which shows the typical structure of a mystery story, from beginning to end, including various clues and plot twists.

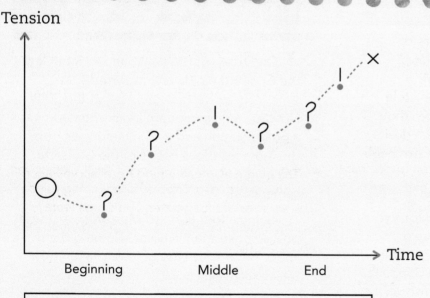

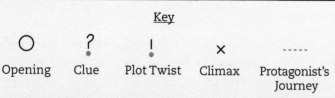

A A wealthy widow, who has recently remarried, is found poisoned.

B Evidence suggests that the widow's stepson had bought poison.

C Witnesses heard the widow arguing with someone shortly before her death.

D The widow's best friend appears to hate the widow's new husband.

E The widow's new husband wasn't there when the widow was poisoned.

F The widow's stepson will inherit everything after the widow's death.

G The widow's new husband was spotted buying poison.

H The widow had recently made a new will but this has gone missing.

Activities

1 Plot the details on page 20 (labelled A–H) from an Agatha Christie story, *The Mysterious Affair at Styles*, onto a graph like the one opposite to show how you would structure this story. Identify the clues and plot twists and think about how you can re-order the details to create the most exciting mystery.

 2 What do you think the climax of the Agatha Christie story will reveal? Write a brief paragraph giving your own solution to the mystery.

3 Read the extract below which describes some of the clues that real-life detectives follow when investigating crimes. Use these clues and your own ideas to help you plan the plot for a new mystery crime story.

↔ **Stretch**

Create a graph showing the plot of a mystery story you have read or seen recently. Compare this to the mystery story graph opposite. What similarities or differences do you notice?

Extract from *Forensics* by Richard Platt

Tell-tale marks

A trail of blood, a cluster of bullet holes or a series of scratches on a window ledge: all of these marks at a crime scene have a story to tell. They are all forms of pattern evidence. Reading and understanding them helps detectives to reconstruct a crime. The shape of the marks and their position can show the way a villain broke into a house, where a killer was standing, and even whether they were right- or left-handed!

The nicks that say 'you're nicked!'

Worn tools have scratches and nicks that make them like no other. When an old crowbar is used to lever open a window, the tool presses into the paintwork a pattern that is as unique as a signature. If police find the crowbar, they can compare its marks with the pattern evidence and accuse its owner.

Arms and ammunition

Guns also tell a story [...] The lead slug fired from the barrel marks or pierces everything it strikes. This pattern shows detectives how the bullet flew. The other part of the bullet, the cartridge case [...] is usually ejected to one side. So the pattern of cases can show where an assassin was standing to shoot.

Charting patterns

Analysing blood marks is a special skill. Detectives chart the angles of splattered drops using ruled lines, threads or a computer. The drops literally point to where the victim was standing when they were wounded.

 **Glossary**

red herrings   false clues that are planted to mislead

21

7 Watching the Detectives

↻ Objective

Explore characterization in extracts from different mystery stories.

You will find many different characters in a mystery story: victims, suspects and villains, but the most important character is often the detective – the person investigating the mystery itself.

✎ Activities

SPAG

1 Discuss what makes a good detective. Choose three **adjectives** from the words on the bottom right and explain why these are important character traits for a detective.

↔ Stretch

Suggest an alternative list of eight adjectives and rank these in order of importance.

The extracts on page 23 feature two very different detectives. The first extract is from the novel *The Big Sleep* by Raymond Chandler about the private investigator Philip Marlowe, while the second extract is from Arthur Conan Doyle's first Sherlock Holmes story, *A Study in Scarlet*.

📖 Glossary

adjective   a word that describes a noun, e.g. *happy*, *blue*, *furious*

brogues   a type of shoe

torpor   inactivity

alluded   hinted

philosophical instruments   scientific equipment

adventurous

cautious

arrogant

conscientious

persistent

quick-witted

rational

risk-taking

Name:
Philip Marlowe

Job title:
Private investigator

....

Extract from
The Big Sleep by
Raymond Chandler

It was about eleven o'clock in the morning, mid October, with the sun not shining and a look of hard wet rain in the clearness of the foothills. I was wearing my powder-blue suit, with dark blue shirt, tie and display handkerchief, black **brogues**, black wool socks with dark blue clocks on them. I was neat, clean, shaven and sober, and I didn't care who knew it. I was everything the well-dressed private detective ought to be. I was calling on four million dollars.

Name:
Sherlock Holmes

Job title:
Consulting detective

....

Extract from
A Study in Scarlet by
Arthur Conan Doyle

In height he was rather over six feet and so excessively lean that he seemed to be considerably taller. His eyes were sharp and piercing, save during those intervals of **torpor** to which I have **alluded**; and his thin hawk-like nose gave his whole expression an air of alertness and decision. His chin, too, had the prominence and squareness which mark the man of determination. His hands were invariably blotted with ink and stained with chemicals, yet he was possessed of extraordinary delicacy of touch, as I frequently had occasion to observe when I watched him manipulating his fragile **philosophical instruments**.

2 What do you learn about each detective from reading these extracts? Think about:

- how Philip Marlowe narrates the story and what this reveals about his character

- how Sherlock Holmes is described and what this suggests about his character.

Select quotations from each extract to support the points you make.

3 Based on these extracts, which story would you want to continue reading? Give reasons for your answer.

4a Create your own fictional detective. Discuss the character traits you could give your detective.

4b Write a 100–150 word description of your fictional detective. Use one of the extracts as a model for your own writing.

Support

Will you make your detective an amateur sleuth, a professional private investigator or a police detective? How might this affect the character traits you give him or her?

More to explore

You can learn about characters in several ways. A writer can reveal:

- physical traits – what the character looks like

- dialogue – what the character says

- actions – what the character does

- point of view – what the character thinks

- how other characters react to them.

The extract on page 25 is from the opening of *The Ruby in the Smoke* by Philip Pullman. Read the extract and then complete the activities below.

✎ Activities continued

5 What do you think the mystery in this story will be? What clues does the opening give you?

6a What do you learn about Sally Lockhart from this extract? Think about:

- how the writer describes her

- what Sally says and does

- how the porter reacts to her.

Select quotations from the extract to support the points you make.

6b An ellipsis (...) can be used to indicate a trailing off into silence. Look again at Sally's dialogue and discuss what the use of ellipses might suggest about her feelings.

SPAG

Extract from
The Ruby in the Smoke
by Philip Pullman

On a cold, fretful afternoon in early October, 1872, a hansom cab drew up outside the offices of Lockhart and Selby, Shipping Agents in the financial heart of London, and a young girl got out and paid the driver.

She was a person of sixteen or so – alone, and uncommonly pretty. She was slender and pale, and dressed in mourning, with a black bonnet under which she tucked back a straying twist of blonde hair that the wind had teased loose. She had unusually dark eyes for one so fair. Her name was Sally Lockhart; and within fifteen minutes, she was going to kill a man.

She stood looking up at the building for a moment, and then climbed the three steps and entered. There was a drab corridor facing her, with a porter's office on the right, where an old man sat in front of a fire reading a Penny Dreadful. She tapped on the glass, and he sat up guiltily, thrusting the magazine down beside his chair.

'Beg pardon, miss,' he said. 'Didn't see yer come in.'

'I've come to see Mr Selby,' she said. 'But he wasn't expecting me.'

'Name, please, miss?'

'My name is Lockhart. My father was... Mr Lockhart.'

He became friendlier at once.

'Miss Sally, is it? You been here before, miss!'

'Have I? I'm sorry, I don't remember...'

'Must've been ten year ago at least. You sat by my fire and had a ginger biscuit and told me all about your pony. You forgotten already? Dear me... I was very sorry to hear about your father, miss. That was a terrible thing, the ship going down like that. He was a real gentleman, miss.'

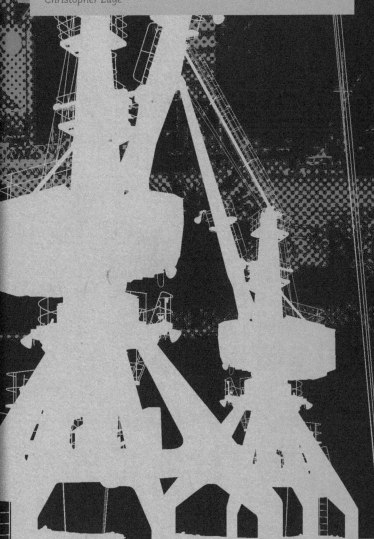

⏰ Extra Time

How might the story continue? Think about how you could reveal more about Sally's character to the reader. Write the next ten lines of the story.

ignite INTERVIEW

'When you get your first spark of inspiration for the story, you have got to keep the excitement about that idea going all the way through the writing, because that will help keep your readers interested.'

Christopher Edge

8 Scene of the Crime

↻ Objective

Explore how writers create effective narrative voices.

When writing a story you have to decide from whose perspective you are going to tell the story. For example, the extract opposite uses the first person plural, 'we'. You could also choose to write in the first person ('I'), second person ('you') or third person ('he'/'she'/'they'). Each of these can have a very different effect on your story and on the way a reader responds to your story. Read the extract on this page from the opening of the novel *The Secret History* by Donna Tartt and then complete the activities that follow.

Extract from *The Secret History* by Donna Tartt

The snow in the mountains was melting and Bunny had been dead for several weeks before we came to understand the gravity of our situation. He'd been dead for ten days before they found him, you know. It was one of the biggest manhunts in Vermont history – state troopers, the FBI, even an army helicopter; the college closed, the dye factory in Hampden shut down, people coming from New Hampshire, upstate New York, as far away as Boston.

It is difficult to believe that Henry's modest plan could have worked so well despite these unforeseen events. We hadn't intended to hide the body where it couldn't be found. In fact, we hadn't hidden it at all but had simply left it where it fell in hopes that some luckless passer-by would stumble over it before anyone even noticed he was missing. This was a tale that told itself simply and well: the loose rocks, the body at the bottom of the ravine with a break in the neck, and the muddy skidmarks of dug-in heels pointing the way down; a hiking accident, no more, no less, and it might have been left at that, at quiet tears and a small funeral, had it not been for the snow that fell that night; it covered him without a trace, and ten days later, when the thaw finally came, the state troopers and the FBI and the searchers from town all saw that they had been walking back and forth over his body until the snow above it was packed down like ice.

CRIME SCENE

Activities

1a Re-read the opening sentence. Who do you think is narrating the story?

1b The extract is written in the first person plural. What effect does this create? Why do you think the writer has chosen to narrate the story from this viewpoint?

SPAG

Support

Mystery stories are often told in the first person so that the reader shares the narrator's viewpoint as they uncover the clues to solve the mystery. How is the use of a first-person viewpoint different in this mystery story?

2 How does the writer build up a sense of place in the extract? Select details and explain the clues these give about the setting. Record your ideas in a grid like the one started below.

3a Re-read the final sentence, which begins 'This was a tale...'. What more do you learn about Bunny's death from this sentence?

3b How does the way the final sentence is structured help to reveal more about the mystery?

4 Rewrite the extract as a **third-person narrative**. How does this change the impact of the opening?

SPAG

Glossary

third-person narrative   when the narrator is not a character in the story and relates the action using third-person pronouns, such as 'he' and 'she'

Details	Clues about setting
'The snow in the mountains was melting...'	This might mean it's springtime...

DO NOT ENTER

9 Step into the Mystery

↺ Objective

Use role-play and creative writing to explore setting and situation.

Mysteries can happen anywhere. Read the extract on this page, from *The London Eye Mystery* by Siobhan Dowd. Ted and Kat are waiting for their cousin Salim to finish his ride on the London Eye.

ignite INTERVIEW

'You can actually set a mystery story anywhere – it is only the ingredients that remain consistent: a detective, clues, suspects, a villain and maybe a twist at the end of the tale.'

Christopher Edge

Extract from *The London Eye Mystery* by Siobhan Dowd

The pod sank slowly to nine o'clock. I remember from the time we'd gone up before how, near the end of the ride, a souvenir photograph is taken automatically. The London Eye managers have fixed a camera into position, so that a good shot of everyone is possible against a backdrop of Big Ben. It happens somewhere between eight and seven o'clock. I saw the dark figures inside Salim's pod gather to one side, facing out northeast to where the camera was. I even made out a flash.

Then we walked to where we'd arranged to meet Salim and waited for his pod to land. At 12.02 precisely it came back to earth. The pod doors opened. A group of six grown-up Japanese tourists came out first. Then came a fat man and woman with their two small boys who were also fat, which probably meant they all ate too much convenience food and needed to improve their diet. The girl in the fluffy jacket followed, arm in arm with her boyfriend. A big burly man in a raincoat, with white hair and a briefcase, came out next. He looked like he should have been getting off a commuter train, not the Eye. And then came a tall, thin blonde lady holding hands with a grey-haired man who was much shorter than her. Finally two African women in flowing, colourful robes came out, laughing like they'd just been at the fun fair. Four children of various ages were with them and they looked very happy.

But of Salim there was no sign.

I knew straight away that something was wrong.

Activities

1 Role-play the police interviewing Ted and Kat after they report Salim missing. Draw on details from the extract in your role-play.

2 What do you think has happened to Salim? Discuss your theories.

3 Choose a photograph of a setting and a photograph of a person from the selection here. Now write a paragraph putting the person into the setting you have chosen. Think about:

- what they are doing there
- what they can see/hear/smell
- how they might be feeling
- what mystery they might discover.

10 Assessment: Writing a Mystery Short Story

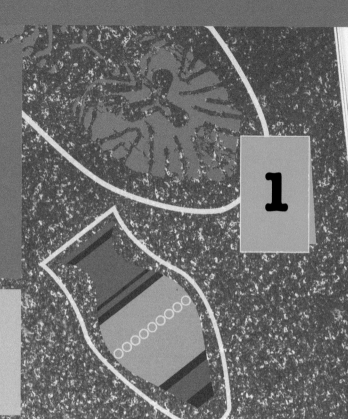

You have been asked to write a short story in the mystery genre. This story will be collected into an e-book anthology of mystery stories and published and sold online. Here is an email from the editors of the anthology.

We're looking for exciting new authors to appear in an e-book anthology of mystery stories. This anthology is going to be aimed at readers aged 12 and older and we're looking for mystery stories that will keep these readers on the edge of their seats.

Your story could be set anywhere in the world, in the past, present or even the future, but it must include the features of a mystery, i.e. a baffling crime or puzzle to be solved, an investigator, suspects and clues, and a final plot twist. The setting and characters are up to you, but the story itself must be no longer than 2000 words.

The editors will be looking for skill in:

- using features of the mystery genre to create an intriguing story
- using a range of sentence structures and vocabulary to create interest
- writing accurate paragraphs and sentences with correct punctuation and spelling.

In particular, they will want to see:

- a consistent use of narrative voice
- the building of tension throughout the story
- a dramatic opening and an ending that resolves the mystery in a satisfying way.

Use what you've learned about the mystery genre to create an original short story that will enthral and intrigue the reader. We look forward to reading your submission.

3

Before you write...

Plan: Use the knowledge and skills you have learned throughout this unit. Think about how you are going to plan your short story, including what makes a dramatic opening, the clues and plot twists you could include, and how the climax to the story will resolve the mystery. Think about the setting of the story and the characters you will include, and how you can make these believable for your readers.

As you write...

Review and edit: Check that you are following your plan, keeping your aims in mind, reading and re-reading what you have written to make sure it makes sense and is creating the effect you want to achieve.

When you have finished writing...

Proofread: Check that what you have written is clear and accurate, with correct punctuation and spelling. Check particularly for errors that you know you tend to make in your writing.

POLICE LINE DO NOT CROSS POLICE LINE DO
NOT CROSS POLICE LINE

2 WORDS OF WAR

How does poetry help us understand the impact of war?

Introduction

When the First World War broke out in 1914, the writer H. G. Wells referred to it as the 'war to end all wars'. However, since then many devastating conflicts have taken place across the globe.

All wars bring change and trauma, and people often turn to poetry as a way of expressing their thoughts and emotions. These emotions can range from fierce patriotism (loyalty to your country) and excitement, to horror, anger and grief.

In this unit, you will find out how poems, particularly First World War poetry, create impact, rouse different emotions and make people reflect on human behaviour in wartime.

ignite INTERVIEW
Ed Boanas, Infantry officer

The First World War is hugely significant in terms of a change to how warfare was conducted, in the scale of the suffering, the endurance and the endeavour and it is very important that it is remembered. My view of war in general is that it is the consequence of differences between nations and other actors that they cannot resolve by peaceful means. It is important to learn from what we have done in past wars, to highlight the thing that doesn't change about war: the fact that it is fought by people and that it comes with pain, and all of the things that everyone knows about war across the centuries. But how wars are fought changes over time.

✎ Activities

1 Write down as many words as you can that spring to mind when you think of war and its associations. Include nouns and verbs. Aim for at least 15, e.g. *hate, fight, blood, charge.*

2 Arrange the words into a short, simple poetic sequence, starting with the word 'War' and ending with the word 'Peace'. You could arrange the words in patterns of sound, such as **alliteration**, **assonance** and **rhyme**, or into a pattern of action or events.

📖 Glossary

alliteration repetition of the same letter or sound at the beginning of words, e.g. *sitting silently*

assonance repetition of the same vowel sounds in neighbouring words, e.g. *breathing beneath the sea*

rhyme when the sounds at the end of words match, usually at the end of lines of poetry, e.g. *Splashing along the boggy woods all day/And over brambled hedge and holding clay*

Joining Up

↻ Objective

Understand how texts reflect the historical context in which they are written.

The first major war to involve millions of ordinary people (and not just soldiers) was the First World War. When war was declared in 1914, many men thought it was an exciting adventure to enlist in the army. Anyone who didn't was given a hard time and many were accused of being cowards. Look carefully at the three recruitment posters on this page.

✎ Activities

1 How do Poster 1 and Poster 2 work? Look at:

- the expressions on the people's faces and the way they are posed

- where each poster is set, the objects we see and the background

- the colours used.

All of these things have been very deliberately chosen. Why?

2 Look at Poster 3. What message do you think it was trying to send to people who saw it? Write your own slogan to reinforce that message. (You can't use 'Your Country Needs You!')

The posters suggest that fighting, even dying, for your country is noble and **patriotic**. The poem below expresses the same viewpoint. It was written at the outbreak of the First World War. Brooke died before he experienced front-line combat.

'The Soldier' by Rupert Brooke

If I should die, think only this of me:

That there's some corner of a foreign field

That is for ever England. There shall be

In that rich earth a richer dust concealed;

A dust whom England bore, shaped, made aware,

Gave, once, her flowers to love, her ways to roam,

A body of England's, breathing English air,

Washed by the rivers, blest by suns of home.

And think, this heart, all evil shed away,

A pulse in the eternal mind, no less

Gives somewhere back the thoughts by England given;

Her sights and sounds; dreams happy as her day;

And laughter, learnt of friends; and gentleness,

In hearts at peace, under an English heaven.

3 What do the following lines suggest that Brooke thinks about dying for your country?

… There shall be

In that rich earth a richer dust concealed

4 Choose another short section of the poem and explain how you think it presents a patriotic view.

📖 Glossary

patriotic devoted to and vigorously supporting one's country

2 At the Front

↻ Objective

Explore how language choices and literary features can create a powerful effect.

Wilfred Owen was another poet writing during the First World War. His poetry was realistic about life in the trenches, and many people found it shocking.

In January 1917, Owen wrote a letter to his mother recounting a recent event in the trenches.

Owen used this experience in his poem 'The Sentry'. Read the extract below.

In the platoon on my left the **sentries** over the dug-out were blown to nothing. One of these poor fellows was my first servant whom I rejected. If I had kept him he would have lived, for servants don't do Sentry Duty. I kept my own sentries half way down the stairs during the more terrific bombardment. In spite of this one lad was blown down and, I'm afraid, blinded.

Extract from 'The Sentry' by Wilfred Owen

There we herded from the blast

Of whizz-bangs, but one found our door at last,

Buffeting eyes and breath, snuffing the candles.

And thud! flump! thud! down the steep steps came thumping

And splashing in the flood, deluging muck —

The sentry's body; then his rifle, handles

Of old Boche bombs, and mud in ruck on ruck.

We dredged him up, for killed, until he whined

'O sir, my eyes — I'm blind — I'm blind, I'm blind!'

Coaxing, I held a flame against his lids

And said if he could see the least blurred light

He was not blind; in time he'd get all right.

'I can't,' he sobbed. Eyeballs, huge-bulged like squids

Watch my dreams still; but I forgot him there

In posting next for duty, and sending a scout

To beg a stretcher somewhere, and floundering about

To other posts under the shrieking air.

Activities

1 Why do you think the poet includes **direct speech** in the poem? Explain your answer using quotations from the poem.

SPAG

2 How do the words 'whined' and 'sobbed' add to our image of the victim?

3 What do we learn about the narrator from how he handles the situation?

4 The poet uses **onomatopoeic** words in the poem, such as 'buffeting'. Pick out five other examples and explain their effect, for example: **The word 'buffeting' describes the blast of air that knocks the soldiers after the explosion of a whizz-bang near their door. The sound of the word echoes the sensation of being hit.**

 Support

When considering the effect of these words, say them aloud and think about their sound.

5 Pick out the **simile** that the poet uses. Explain the image it creates and its effect on the reader.

📖 **Glossary**

direct speech words, within inverted commas in a sentence, actually spoken by someone

onomatopoeia using a word that imitates what it stands for, e.g. *crash*

simile a comparison of one thing with another which uses the words 'like' or 'as', e.g. *The shadowy figure stood as still as a tombstone.*

☑ **Progress Check**

In a short paragraph, explain how the poet uses language to create powerful effects, using close reference to the text.

Swap your paragraph with a partner. Give your partner's paragraph a rating on a scale of 1 to 3 (with 3 being the highest) on how well they have:

- picked out specific words, phrases or literary features
- explained the effects that they create for the reader.

🕐 **Extra Time**

Research 'Dulce et Decorum Est', one of Wilfred Owen's most famous poems. At the end it states 'The old Lie'. What is the lie?

③ Keeping a Diary

↻ Objective

Appreciate the use of editing skills in order to make a text clear, informative and interesting for a reader.

Many of the soldiers who fought in the First World War kept diaries. Below are two extracts from Captain Alexander Stewart's war diary.

June 2, 1916

The dugouts in this part of the line were infested with rats. They would frequently walk over one when asleep. I was much troubled by them coming and licking the **brilliantine** off my hair; for this reason, I had to give up using grease on my head. I never heard them biting anyone.

Nov 9, 1916

I am very much annoyed by memos sent round from Headquarters that come in at all hours of the day and night; they stop me getting a full night's rest and some of them are very silly and quite unnecessary. When I am very tired and just getting off to sleep with cold feet, in comes an orderly with a **chit** asking how many pairs of socks my company had a week ago; I reply '141 and a half'. I then go to sleep; back comes a memo: 'Please explain at once how you come to be **deficient** of one sock'. I reply 'man lost his leg'. That's how we make the **Huns** sit up.

✎ Activities

1 Stewart survived the war but suffered what we now call post-traumatic stress disorder. What do these extracts tell us about his way of coping with the horror of war at the time? Explain your answer with close reference to the text.

2 Both diary extracts make use of a range of punctuation. What sorts of punctuation are used and for what purposes? For example, what punctuation marks are used to separate independent clauses that are closely linked to each other in sense?

SPAG

📖 Glossary

brilliantine   scented oil used on men's hair to make it look glossy and hold it in place

chit   note

deficient   lacking

Huns   slang for German soldiers

June 7, 1916

We left our billets and went to the edge of the village, moving undercover of the broken walls, then entered a communication trench called 'Yale Street', moved along this trench in daylight for 300yds and then were only 100yds from our own front line and 400yds from the enemy front line, this 'com' trench was in places only 3ft deep, and we were exposed to the enemy fire and our own work was to deepen this trench to 7ft, also make it wide enough for two men to pass, no earth could be thrown on top, but had to be put in sandbags and passed down the trench.

Everything went well 'till 3 o'clock in the afternoon when Jerry started to strafe and strafed us away from work, and managed it without any casualties, during the time we were working we had to keep our equipment on, also rifles at hand, and leaving the trench we looked 'rum cutters' being covered with mud and clay.

3 Fred's diary is to be published, but it needs editing. Use your skills to:

SPAG

- add punctuation to make the text easier to read
- delete, add or change some words, so that the meaning is clearer
- vary the sentence lengths, to make the writing style more interesting
- look up and explain unfamiliar words.

4 If Fred were alive today, list some questions that you might ask him in order to describe his experience in more detail.

The following extract is taken from the diary of Thomas Frederick Littler, known as Fred, who joined up shortly after his 17th birthday. He describes his experience of battle in Northern France.

4 Class War

↺ Objective

Explore the layers of meaning in a poem, identifying euphemisms and irony.

Siegfried Sassoon served as an officer in France during the First World War. At first he was eager to fight for his country, but as the war progressed his attitude changed. In 1917, he said in a letter to his commanding officer: 'I believe that the war upon which I entered as a war of defence and liberation has become a war of aggression and conquest.'

It wasn't just the motives behind the war that Sassoon doubted. Read the poem below to discover what else Sassoon resented about the war effort.

📖 Glossary

squire   local landowner who employed people to work on his land

Lord Derby's scheme   recruitment scheme proposed by Lord Derby that encouraged men to put their names on a list, on the understanding they would only be called to fight if they were needed

Passchendaele   battle in which both sides suffered huge losses

gilded   covered with a layer of gold

'Memorial Tablet' by Siegfried Sassoon

Squire nagged and bullied till I went to fight,
(Under **Lord Derby's scheme**). I died in hell –
(They called it **Passchendaele**). My wound was slight,
And I was hobbling back; and then a shell
Burst slick upon the duckboards: so I fell
Into the bottomless mud, and lost the light.

At sermon-time, while Squire is in his pew,
He gives my **gilded** name a thoughtful stare;
For, though low down upon the list, I'm there;
'In proud and glorious memory'... that's my due.
Two bleeding years I fought in France, for Squire:
I suffered anguish that he's never guessed.
I came home on leave: and then went west...
What greater glory could a man desire?

Activities

1a What do we learn about the fictional narrator of this poem?

1b What do we learn about the Squire in the poem?

1c Explain the meaning of the phrases 'lost the light' and 'went west' in your own words. Why does the narrator use these **euphemisms**?

1d How do the words 'hell' and 'anguish' contrast with the words 'glory' and 'proud'? Which words does the narrator think are most appropriate to describe his experience?

1e How does the narrator use **irony** in the final line?

2a As part of a series remembering the First World War, your local TV station is recording actors reciting some war poems. You have been commissioned to film a sequence of images to accompany Sassoon's 'Memorial Tablet', as it is read aloud.

First, read through the poem carefully, making notes of the sort of visual images you think might appear on the screen as the words are read.

2b Share your ideas with a partner or group. Decide on the best ones to accompany each small section of the poem.

Glossary

euphemism   substituted word or phrase for something that is unpleasant or embarrassing

irony   saying something that is the opposite of what you mean, often for humorous effect

Progress Check

Recite the poem 'Memorial Tablet', varying your tone, intonation, volume and pace to reflect the mood of the different lines. Plan and rehearse it first, using your voice to emphasize the meaning of the different parts.

Ask your audience to rate your delivery in marks out of 5 (with 5 being the highest). Invite them to suggest one area of improvement.

ignite INTERVIEW

'Poetry can convey emotion, a sense of place, and touch to the individual feelings of people. For the people involved in warfare, it is a hugely involving and engaging business.'

Ed Boanas

5 Revealing Character

↻ Objective

Explore how characterization can reinforce the theme of a poem.

Siegfried Sassoon often took small incidents from his experience at the front line to inspire his poems. In his diary, he described a visit by a senior officer to the camp where men were waiting to be sent to the front line trenches.

A Brigadier-General came and sat down a few feet away. He had the puffy, petulant face of a man with a liver who spends most of the year sitting in London clubs. He began guzzling **hors-d'oeuvres** as though his life depended on the solidity of his meal.

📖 Glossary

hors d'oeuvre small savoury snack eaten before a main meal

A few days later he added another comment to his diary entry, addressed directly to the officer.

You will guzzle yourself to the grave and gas about the Great War long after I am dead with all my promise unfulfilled.

✎ Activities

1a What is Sassoon's opinion of the Brigadier-General? Use words and phrases from the diary to explain your answer.

1b What does the poet mean by the phrase 'my promise unfulfilled'?

1c How would you describe the mood or tone of the diary entry?

'Base Details'
by Siegfried Sassoon

If I were fierce, and bald, and short of breath

I'd live with scarlet Majors at the Base,

And speed glum heroes up the line to death.

You'd see me with my puffy petulant face,

Guzzling and gulping in the best hotel,

Reading the Roll of Honour. 'Poor young chap,'

I'd say — 'I used to know his father well;

Yes, we've lost heavily in this last scrap.'

And when the war is done and youth stone dead,

I'd toddle safely home and die — in bed.

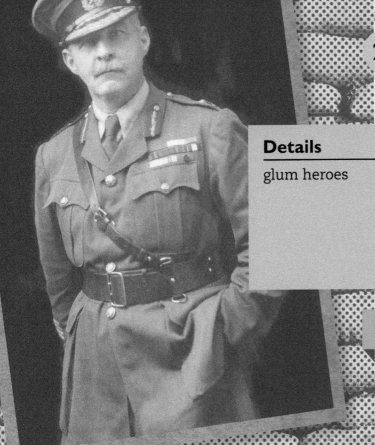

2a How does the poem 'Base Details' echo the ideas and words in the diary entry?

2b The characterization of the 'scarlet Majors' is very powerful. What effect do you think Sassoon wanted to have on the reader when he used the following:
- 'bald, and short of breath'
- 'guzzling and gulping'
- 'toddle safely home'
- 'die – in bed'?

2c What does the direct speech tell us about the attitude of the 'scarlet Majors'?

2d How does the poet use alliteration to emphasize some images in the text?

2e Look at the references to ordinary soldiers and explain what effect they have on the reader. Record your ideas in a grid like the one started below.

Details	Effect they create
glum heroes	The word 'glum' suggests the soldiers are reluctant, quiet and unhappy, even though they are regarded as 'heroes' because they are going into battle. It makes the reader doubt that the soldiers see themselves as 'heroes'.

↔ Stretch

Write a second stanza as a soldier beginning 'But I am…'.

6 Painting the War

↻ **Objective**

Plan and draft a poem based on the mood and atmosphere created in a painting.

Paul Nash

Two of the best-known artists who painted images of the First World War are the British artist Paul Nash and the German artist Otto Dix.

Nash fought in France but was wounded and returned to the front as an official war artist. Dix was a soldier who fought in France and Russia but suffered post-traumatic stress disorder. He had nightmares all his life about the terrifying experiences he had on the battlefield.

Look carefully at the two paintings (on this page and on page 45).

✎ Activities

1a What do you think happened immediately before these scenes and what might happen immediately after?

1b Jot down some words that you think sum up the mood of each painting.

1c How does the use of colour and light and dark add to the mood in each painting?

1d Write a suitable title or caption for each of these paintings.

1e What other scenes do these paintings remind you of? It could be other paintings or photographs, films, video games or maybe even TV or Internet advertisements.

1f If there were speech or thought bubbles for any of the people in the paintings, what would they say?

Otto Dix

2a Choose one of the paintings to use as the subject of a short poem.

2b Using your responses to Activities 1a–1f, select some key words to include in your poem.

2c Decide whether to use one of the characters in your painting to narrate your poem.

2d Try to build up a powerful mood in your reader's mind, by using strong, descriptive imagery, including colours, light and dark, a sense of movement or stillness, the emotions of the characters, etc.

2e Write the first draft of your poem. Read it aloud. Improve it by:

- experimenting with different word choices

- altering the lengths of the lines for maximum impact (e.g. short lines can emphasize a particular word or thought)

- considering alternative imagery

- changing words or phrases to improve the sound of the poem.

🕐 **Extra Time**

If you saw both paintings in a gallery and knew nothing about them, which do you think would be most modern? Explain your answer carefully.

7 Rhythms of War

↺ Objective

Explore how patterns of language and sound can reinforce the theme of a poem.

Drums have been linked with battle since primitive times. The beating of rhythms has been used for marching, rallying troops and ceremony. Different rhythms reflect different occasions and emotions. Slow steady beats can reinforce a sense of order and unity, whereas fast beats reflect excitement and tension.

In poetry, the term 'rhythm' describes the pattern of light and heavy beats (stresses) on syllables in a line.

✎ Activities

1a Read aloud the first three stanzas from 'The Charge of the Light Brigade'. What do you think is being described? Explain your answer with close reference to the text.

1b Think about the patterns of sound in the poem and its rhythms. Explain how they help to create a sense of tension and drama.

1c What do you think the poet feels about 'the six hundred'? Explain which words in the poem show this.

'The Charge of the Light Brigade' by Alfred Lord Tennyson

I
Half a league, half a league,
    Half a league onward,
All in the valley of Death
    Rode the six hundred.
'Forward, the Light Brigade!
Charge for the guns!' he said:
Into the valley of Death
    Rode the six hundred.

II
'Forward, the Light Brigade!'
Was there a man dismay'd?
Not tho' the soldier knew
    Some one had blunder'd:
Their's not to make reply,
Their's not to reason why,
Their's but to do and die:
Into the valley of Death
    Rode the six hundred.

III
Cannon to right of them,
Cannon to left of them,
Cannon in front of them
    Volley'd and thunder'd;
Storm'd at with shot and shell,
Boldly they rode and well,
Into the jaws of Death,
Into the mouth of Hell
    Rode the six hundred.

IV

Flash'd all their sabres bare,
Flash'd as they turn'd in air
Sabring the gunners there,
Charging an army, while
    All the world wonder'd:
Plunged in the battery-smoke
Right thro' the line they broke;
Cossack and Russian
Reel'd from the sabre-stroke
    Shatter'd and sunder'd.
Then they rode back, but not
    Not the six hundred.

V

Cannon to right of them,
Cannon to left of them,
Cannon behind them
    Volley'd and thunder'd;
Stormed at with shot and shell,
While horse and hero fell,
They that had fought so well
Came thro' the jaws of Death,
Back from the mouth of Hell,
All that was left of them,
    Left of six hundred.

VI

When can their glory fade?
O the wild charge they made!
    All the world wonder'd.
Honour the charge they made!
Honour the Light Brigade,
    Noble six hundred!

2 Read the remaining three stanzas aloud. What do you learn from this part of the poem?

3 In groups, prepare a performance of 'The Charge of the Light Brigade'. Consider:

- how to convey the mood of the poem
- whether different voices should read different sections
- how to draw attention to important words
- what pace and volume are appropriate
- whether you want to add any sound effects or actions to the reading.

Prepare to explain your performance choices and to answer questions on your understanding of the poem.

4 Perform your poem. Ask your audience to give you a rating on a scale of 1 to 5 (with 5 being the highest) on the impact of your performance. Then ask them to comment on two aspects they thought you did well and one aspect that you could improve. Finally, take some questions from the audience on your performance choices and your understanding of the poem.

ignite INTERVIEW

"The Charge of the Light Brigade' is probably one of the greatest examples of a military order not given clearly, clearly misunderstood.'

Ed Boanas

8 Shaping the Message

↻ Objective

Understand how the structure of a poem helps to convey its meaning.

A poem differs from prose because it has a certain shape on the page. The poet decides when to end one line and start the next. The shape of the poem influences which lines and words have most impact, where we pause and where images start and finish.

A haiku is a Japanese-style poem that has strict rules about shape:

- It has just three lines.
- The first and last lines have five syllables.
- The middle line has seven syllables.

✎ Activities

1 Lay out the text below in the form of a haiku, using the rules above.

The fight for freedom won't end 'til we teach children love instead of hate.

2 How does the structure of a haiku strengthen its message for the reader?

3 Choose one of the wartime pictures on the right and write a haiku to capture the mood or tone in the picture.

📖 Glossary

reverence worship

ornament decoration

epic long, historical

paddies rice fields

rhetorical question a question asked for effect that doesn't require an answer

Denise Levertov wrote many anti-war poems, including the one below, which mourned the damage done in Vietnam by American bomb attacks.

'What Were They Like?'
by Denise Levertov

1) Did the people of Viet Nam
   use lanterns of stone?

2) Did they hold ceremonies
   to **reverence** the opening of buds?

3) Were they inclined to quiet laughter?

4) Did they use bone and ivory,
   jade and silver, for **ornament**?

5) Had they an **epic** poem?

6) Did they distinguish between speech and singing?

1) Sir, their light hearts turned to stone.
   It is not remembered whether in gardens
   stone lanterns illumined pleasant ways.

2) Perhaps they gathered once to delight in blossom,
   but after their children were killed
   there were no more buds.

3) Sir, laughter is bitter to the burned mouth.

4) A dream ago, perhaps. Ornament is for joy.
   All the bones were charred.

5) It is not remembered. Remember,
   most were peasants; their life
   was in rice and bamboo.
   When peaceful clouds were reflected in the **paddies**
   and the water buffalo stepped surely along terraces,
   maybe fathers told their sons old tales.
   When bombs smashed those mirrors
   there was time only to scream.

6) There is an echo yet
   of their speech which was like a song.
   It was reported their singing resembled
   the flight of moths in moonlight.
   Who can say? It is silent now.

4a There are two speakers in the poem. How do you know this? Which lines are delivered by which speaker?

4c What does the final question in the poem mean? Is it a **rhetorical question**?

4b What do you notice about the structure of the questions and answers? What is the significance of the word 'Sir'?

4d The poet compares images of peace and beauty with images of violence. Choose two examples and explain what effect this comparison has on the reader.

9 Aftermath

↻ Objective

Consider the effect of rhyme and imagery.

The legacy of war is often one of devastation, trauma and exhaustion. The novel *All Quiet on the Western Front* describes the extreme physical and mental stress endured by German soldiers in the First World War and their struggle to adapt to life afterwards. The author, Erich Maria Remarque, said the book aimed to 'simply tell of a generation of men, who even though they may have escaped shells, were destroyed by the war'.

All Quiet on the Western Front by Erich Maria Remarque

The summer of 1918 is the most bloody and the most terrible. The days stand like angels in blue and gold, incomprehensible, above the ring of annihilation. Every man here knows that we are losing the war. Not much is said about it, we are falling back, we will not be able to attack again after this big offensive, we have no more men and no more ammunition.

Still the campaign goes on – the dying goes on –

✎ Activities

1a From the description in the extract, sum up the soldier's feelings as the end of the war nears.

1b What image does he use to describe the endless round of death and destruction? What is the effect of this image?

Other poets have looked at the effects of war from a wider perspective – from the point of view of Nature, which moves forward regardless of what people do.

'There Will Come Soft Rains' by Sara Teasdale

There will come soft rains and the smell of the ground,
And swallows circling with their shimmering sound;

And frogs in the pools singing at night,
And wild plum trees in tremulous white;

Robins will wear their feathery fire,
Whistling their whims on a low fence-wire;

And not one will know of the war, not one
Will care at last when it is done.

Not one would mind, neither bird nor tree,
If mankind perished utterly;

And Spring herself, when she woke at dawn
Would scarcely know that we were gone.

2a What is the poet predicting would happen 'If mankind perished utterly'? Do you feel this is an optimistic (positive) or pessimistic (negative) idea?

2b How does the poet use **personification** to add to the impact of her message?

2c The poem is written in rhyming couplets. Why do you think the poet uses a **half-rhyme** at the end of the poem? What effect does this have?

3 Write a four- or six-line poem, using rhyming couplets, inspired by the picture of the children below. The title of the poem should be 'Aftermath'.

📖 Glossary

personification type of imagery in which living qualities are assigned to inanimate objects

half-rhyme words that have a similar sound but do not rhyme completely

ignite INTERVIEW

'There can be good or bad reasons for going to war, but it is important that both activity and inactivity are weighed up in taking such decisions. Trying to predict what threats we might face in the future is how we try to take forward the learning from the past.'

Ed Boanas

10 Assessment: Reading and Assessing War Poems for an Exhibition

You have been asked to select a war poem that could be given to an artist as inspiration for an illustration. The poem that you choose, and its illustration, will be displayed at an exhibition of war poetry and pictures.

Read all three poems on pages 53–55 carefully. Then select the one that you feel is most suitable for illustration and display. You will need to explain the reasons for your choice to the director of the gallery, in the form of a report.

EXHIBITION THIS WAY

Before you choose…

Consider the questions below as you read the poems.

- What is this poem about? As well as the obvious 'surface layer' of meaning, look deeper to understand what the poet might be implying.

- What feelings does the poet show about the subject?

- How would you describe the mood of the poem?

- What imagery is used and how does this reflect the meaning of the poem?

- Does the poem have a clear beginning/middle/end structure or does it work in a different way?

- Is there a distinctive tone of voice or narrator in the poem?

- What are the most interesting language choices in the poem?

When you have chosen…

Write a report for the gallery director, analysing your chosen poem and explaining why you have chosen it.

Remember that, for a report, you will need to:

- use **Standard English**
- write in the third person, using 'he', 'she' and 'it' for example (except when expressing a personal viewpoint)
- start with an introductory paragraph
- group your ideas into separate paragraphs
- make use of appropriate sub-headings.

Note that, for the purposes of this assessment, you will be marked on your reading and analysis skills, rather than on your writing skills.

📖 Glossary

Standard English   the variety of English that is regarded as 'correct' and is used in more formal situations. It is not specific to any geographical area and can be spoken or written.

Poem 1

'Children in Wartime'
by Isobel Thrilling

Sirens ripped open   *hook*
the warm silk of sleep;

we richocheted to the shelter

moated by streets

that ran with darkness.

People said it was a storm,

but flak

had not the right sound

for rain;

thunder left such huge craters

of silence,

we knew this was no giant

playing bowls.

And later,

when I saw the jaw of glass,

where once had hung

my window spun with stars;

it seemed the sky

lay broken on my floor.

More to explore

53

Poem 2

'War Girls' by Jessie Pope

There's the girl who clips your ticket for the train,

And the girl who speeds the lift from floor to floor,

There's the girl who does a milk-round in the rain,

And the girl who calls for orders at your door.

Strong, sensible, and fit,

They're out to show their grit,

And tackle jobs with energy and knack.

No longer caged and penned up,

They're going to keep their end up

Till the khaki soldier boys come marching back.

There's the motor girl who drives a heavy van,

There's the butcher girl who brings your joint of meat,

There's the girl who cries 'All fares, please!' like a man,

And the girl who whistles taxis up the street.

Beneath each uniform

Beats a heart that's soft and warm,

Though of canny mother-wit they show no lack;

But a solemn statement this is,

They've no time for love and kisses

Till the khaki soldier boys come marching back.

Poem 3

Extract from 'Out of the Blue' by Simon Armitage

You have picked me out.
Through a distant shot of a building burning
you have noticed now
that a white cotton shirt is twirling, turning.

In fact I am waving, waving.
Small in the clouds, but waving, waving.
Does anyone see
a soul worth saving?

So when will you come?
Do you think you are watching, watching
a man shaking crumbs
or pegging out washing?

I am trying and trying.
The heat behind me is bullying, driving,
but the white of surrender is not yet flying.
I am not at the point of leaving, diving.

A bird goes by.
The depth is appalling. Appalling
that others like me
should be wind-milling, wheeling, spiralling, falling.

Are your eyes believing,
believing
that here in the gills
I am breathing.

But tiring, tiring.
Sirens below are wailing, firing.
My arms are numb and my nerves are sagging.
Do you see me, my love. I am failing, flagging.

3

APPEARANCE AND REALITY

How do writers explore the differences between appearance and reality for dramatic effect?

Introduction

How things appear to be doesn't always reflect how they really are. Authors, poets and playwrights often explore the differences between appearance and reality for dramatic effect and use their skills to reveal hidden truths.

In this unit, you will read stories of illusion and mistaken identity, explore how writers use puns and **metaphors** to entertain and illuminate, and trace how this theme has been used by writers across the centuries.

ignite *INTERVIEW*
Debbie Korley, Actress and RSC practitioner

You don't want a book to tell you exactly what it is about right at the beginning. You want to be drawn into the story. You want to be taken on an adventure and that is what we love about theatre. We like being taken on this adventure which is usually very fraught and that is what grips us as an audience and is why nothing is quite how it seems. Appearing in a Shakespeare play is very special because Shakespeare is so universal. We are flawed as human beings and we like to see the flaws and that is what is lovely about Shakespeare.

✏ Activities

1 Think about a time when you told a lie. How did you try to convince others that what you said was the truth?

2 Tell your partner three things about yourself that they do not know. Two of these things should be true, but the other one should be invented. Ask your partner if they can work out which one is not true.

📖 Glossary

metaphor describing something as something else, not meant to be taken literally, e.g. *You are a star.*

① Writing the Illusion

↻ Objective

Analyse and interpret how character and setting are created.

In fiction, a good writer can conjure pictures of characters and settings in a reader's mind. In the extract from Erin Morgenstern's novel *The Night Circus* on page 59, a young boy called Bailey is exploring a mysterious circus and has entered the **illusionist's** tent.

◈ Activities

1 You have been asked to design the set for a stage adaptation of this book. Create a diagram of the illusionist's tent. Make sure you show:

- where the entrance is
- how the seats are arranged
- where Bailey and the illusionist are seated
- the position of the chair that appears to catch fire.

↔ Stretch

How could you create the illusion of the disappearing entrance and the chair that catches fire?

2 How does the writer create a picture of the illusionist in your mind? Discuss the adverbs, adjectives, and **similes** used to describe the illusionist's actions, appearance and props. What impressions do these create?

SPAG

Support

Comment on what the following similes suggest:

- 'a long piece of black silk that ripples like water over the chair'
- 'an ensemble that looks like a ball gown fashioned out of the night sky'.

Think about the **connotations** of the words chosen.

3 Imagine you are the author of *The Night Circus*. Write an email to the actors playing the parts of Bailey and the illusionist, giving advice on how they should play the parts. You should include details from the extract to support the advice you give.

Extract from *The Night Circus* by Erin Morgenstern

Inside it is lit by a line of black iron **sconces** along the rounded wall and contains nothing but a ring of plain wooden chairs. There are only about twenty of them, in two staggered rows so that the view from each seat is comparable. Bailey chooses a seat in the inside row, across from the entrance.

The rest of the seats fill quickly, save for two: the one to his immediate left and another across the circle.

Bailey notices two things at once.

First, that he can no longer see where the entrance had been. The space where the audience had entered now appears to be a solid wall, seamlessly blending with the rest of the tent.

Second, there is now a dark-haired woman in a black coat sitting to his left. He is certain that she was not there before the door disappeared.

Then his attention is removed from both of these events as the empty chair across the circle bursts into flames.

The panic is instant. Those occupying the chairs closest to the flaming chair abandon their seats and rush for the door, only to find that there is no longer a door to be found, only a solid wall.

The flames grow steadily higher, staying close to the chair, licking around the wood, though it does not appear to be burning.

Bailey looks again at the woman to his left, and she winks at him before standing and walking to the centre of the circle. Amidst the panic, she calmly unbuttons her coat and removes it, tossing it with a delicate gesture towards the burning chair.

What had been a heavy wool coat becomes a long piece of black silk that ripples like water over the chair. The flames vanish. Only a few lingering wisps of smoke remain, along with the sharp smell of charred wood that is slowly changing to the comforting scent of a fireplace, tinged with something like cinnamon or clove.

The woman, standing in the centre of the circle of chairs, pulls back the black silk with a flourish, revealing a still-intact chair on which now perch several snow-white doves.

Another flourish, and the black silk folds and curves in on itself, becoming a top hat. The woman places it on her head, topping off an ensemble that looks like a ball gown fashioned out of the night sky: black silk dotted with sparkling white crystals. She acknowledges her audience with a subtle bow.

The illusionist has made her entrance.

📖 Glossary

illusionist a magician who performs visual tricks

simile a comparison which uses the words 'like' or 'as'

connotation the underlying ideas and feelings suggested by a word

sconces decorative brackets used to hold candles

2 Unreliable Narrators

↻ Objective

Explore the role of the unreliable narrator in fiction.

In a first-person narrative, the events of a story are recounted from one character's point of view – the narrator, using 'I'. But can the reader always trust a narrator to tell the truth? An **unreliable narrator** might exaggerate things, miss out important details or even be incapable of telling the truth. In the extract from the opening of Edgar Allan Poe's short story 'The Tell-Tale Heart' on page 61, the narrator attempts to convince the reader that he is not mad.

📖 Glossary

unreliable narrator a narrator whose perspective on events cannot be trusted

acute sharp

hearken listen

foresight care for the future

dissimulation concealing the truth

✎ Activities

1a Read the extract carefully and pick out any clues that suggest that the narrator might be an unreliable narrator. Discuss:

- how he tries to convince the reader that he isn't mad
- the way he describes his thoughts and actions and the information he provides.

1b What do the writer's choice of sentence structure and use of punctuation suggest about the narrator's state of mind?

SPAG

2 Why do you think Edgar Allan Poe chose a first-person narrative to tell this story? Discuss the following reasons and decide which you agree with:

- It allows the reader to understand the narrator's motives for committing the crime.
- The reader 'sees' the story through the narrator's eyes and this adds to the horror.
- It reads like a confession and this helps to build a sense of tension.

Extract from 'The Tell-Tale Heart' by Edgar Allan Poe

TRUE! – nervous – very, very dreadfully nervous I had been and am; but why will you say that I am mad? The disease had sharpened my senses – not destroyed – not dulled them. Above all was the sense of hearing **acute**. I heard all things in the heaven and in the earth. I heard many things in hell. How, then, am I mad? **Hearken**! and observe how healthily – how calmly I can tell you the whole story.

It is impossible to say how first the idea entered my brain; but once conceived, it haunted me day and night. Object there was none. Passion there was none. I loved the old man. He had never wronged me. He had never given me insult. For his gold I had no desire. I think it was his eye! yes, it was this! He had the eye of a vulture – a pale blue eye, with a film over it. Whenever it fell upon me, my blood ran cold; and so by degrees – very gradually – I made up my mind to take the life of the old man, and thus rid myself of the eye forever.

Now this is the point. You fancy me mad. Madmen know nothing. But you should have seen me. You should have seen how wisely I proceeded – with what caution – with what **foresight** – with what **dissimulation** I went to work! I was never kinder to the old man than during the whole week before I killed him.

More to explore

Stories can also be told from the point of view of characters who don't fully understand what is happening around them. Set during the Second World War, the novel *The Boy in the Striped Pyjamas* is told from the perspective of a nine-year-old German boy called Bruno, whose father is the Commandant of Auschwitz Concentration Camp. In the extract on page 63, Bruno describes the view from his bedroom window of the camp on the other side of the fence.

Activities continued

3 Pick out details from the text and explain how these show that Bruno doesn't understand the situation he is living in.

4 Discuss why you think John Boyne chose to write this story from the point of view of a **naïve** nine-year-old boy.

Support

The Boy in the Striped Pyjamas is a children's book. How might this have influenced the writer's decision?

Stretch

Using your own words, write a paragraph explaining what an unreliable narrator is. Give examples from the extracts you have read to support your explanation.

Extract from
The Boy in the Striped Pyjamas by John Boyne

It was as if it were another city entirely, the people all living and working together side by side with the house where he lived. And were they really so different? All the people in the camp wore the same clothes, those pyjamas and their striped cloth caps too; and all the people who wandered through his house (with the exception of Mother, Gretel and him) wore uniforms of varying quality and decoration and caps and helmets with bright red-and-black armbands and carried guns and always looked terribly stern, as if it was all very important really and no one should think otherwise.

What exactly was the difference? he wondered to himself. And who decided which people wore the striped pyjamas and which people wore the uniforms?

Of course sometimes the two groups mixed. He'd often seen the people from his side of the fence on the other side of the fence, and when he watched it was clear that they were in charge. The pyjama people all jumped to attention whenever the soldiers approached and sometimes they fell to the ground and sometimes they didn't even get up and had to be carried away instead.

It's funny that I've never wondered about those people, Bruno thought. And it's funny that when you think of all the times the soldiers go over there – and he had even seen Father go over there on many occasions – that none of them had ever been invited back to the house.

ignite *INTERVIEW*

'When things are put down or in front of us, when things are black and white, it is not as interesting as seeing all the shades of grey that go between that.'

Debbie Korley

🕐 Extra Time

Read all of 'The Tell-Tale Heart'. What is your reaction to it?

📖 Glossary

naïve lacking experience or understanding

③ Looking Differently

↻ Objective

Investigate how and why writers use extended metaphors.

Writers use **figurative language** to make readers see familiar things in new ways. Read the following extract from T. S. Eliot's poem 'The Love Song of J. Alfred Prufrock' where an **extended metaphor** is used to describe the movement of fog.

Extract from 'The Love Song of J. Alfred Prufrock' by T. S. Eliot

The yellow fog that rubs its back upon the window-panes,

The yellow smoke that rubs its muzzle on the window-panes,

Licked its tongue into the corners of the evening,

Lingered upon the pools that stand in drains,

Let fall upon its back the soot that falls from chimneys,

Slipped by the terrace, made a sudden leap,

And seeing that it was a soft October night,

Curled once about the house, and fell asleep.

📖 Glossary

figurative language   words and phrases used to enhance meaning, e.g. using simile or metaphor to make comparisons

extended metaphor   a metaphor that is introduced and then developed in a piece of writing

✎ Activities

1a Discuss what the poet is comparing the fog to. Think about:

- the images he uses to create the extended metaphor

- why he might think the fog shares those qualities.

1b Create your own extended metaphor by comparing another type of weather with a different animal, e.g. the wind as a puppy, etc.

'A Poison Tree'
by William Blake

I was angry with my friend:

I told my wrath, my **wrath** did end.

I was angry with my **foe**:

I told it not, my wrath did grow.

And I watered it in fears,

Night and morning with my tears:

And I sunned it with smiles,

And with soft deceitful **wiles**.

And it grew both day and night.

Till it bore an apple bright.

And my foe beheld it shine,

And he knew that it was mine.

And into my garden stole,

When the night had **veiled the pole**;

In the morning glad I see;

My foe outstretched beneath the tree.

Extended metaphors can help readers understand feelings and emotions in new ways too. Read the poem 'A Poison Tree' on the right and then complete the activities below.

2a What is your initial reaction to this poem? What emotion is William Blake writing about in this poem? What is the extended metaphor he uses to describe this?

2b Discuss how the following images help develop the extended metaphor:

- 'my wrath did grow'
- 'I watered it in fears'
- 'I sunned it with smiles'
- 'Till it bore an apple bright'.

3 Now have a go at creating a new poem using an original extended metaphor.

☑ Progress Check

Read your poem to a partner, group or to the whole class. Prepare to take questions on your poem and then decide, having heard other poems, how successful you feel your poem was. What would you change in your poem and why?

📖 Glossary

wrath vindictive anger

foe enemy

wiles devious strategies

veiled the pole hidden the pole star

4 Wordplay and Puns

↻ Objective

Consider how puns and other forms of wordplay can be used to create humour.

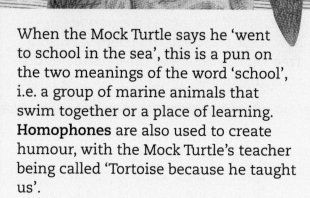

What people say isn't always what they mean. Writers can use the confusion created by **puns** and other forms of wordplay to entertain readers and create humorous effects. Read the extract below from *Alice's Adventures in Wonderland* where Alice is talking to the Mock Turtle.

Extract from *Alice's Adventures in Wonderland* by Lewis Carroll

'When we were little,' the Mock Turtle went on at last, more calmly, though still sobbing a little now and then, 'we went to school in the sea. The master was an old Turtle – we used to call him Tortoise –'

'Why did you call him Tortoise, if he wasn't one?' Alice asked.

'We called him Tortoise because he taught us,' said the Mock Turtle angrily. 'Really you are very dull!'

When the Mock Turtle says he 'went to school in the sea', this is a pun on the two meanings of the word 'school', i.e. a group of marine animals that swim together or a place of learning. **Homophones** are also used to create humour, with the Mock Turtle's teacher being called 'Tortoise because he taught us'.

Now read the extract on page 67 where the Mock Turtle tells Alice about the subjects he studied at school, and complete the activities below.

✎ Activities

1 Match each subject the Mock Turtle mentions to its equivalent in the real world, e.g. 'reeling and writhing' is reading and writing.

2 What is your reaction to the Lewis Carroll extracts? How far does the wordplay add to the reader's interest?

3 Create a list of puns based on the subjects you study at school. Use these puns to create a comic script of a conversation between two new students discussing their school timetable.

Extract from *Alice's Adventures in Wonderland* by Lewis Carroll

'Reeling and Writhing, of course, to begin with,' the Mock Turtle replied; 'And then the different branches of Arithmetic – Ambition, Distraction, Uglification, and Derision.'

'I've never heard of "Uglification",' Alice ventured to say. 'What is it?'

The **Gryphon** lifted up both its paws in surprise. 'Never heard of uglifying!' it exclaimed. 'You know what to beautify is, I suppose?'

'Yes,' said Alice doubtfully: 'it means – to – make – anything – prettier.'

'Well, then,' the Gryphon went on, 'if you don't know what to uglify is, you are a simpleton.'

Alice did not feel encouraged to ask any more questions about it: so she turned to the Mock Turtle, and said 'What else had you to learn?'

'Well, there was Mystery,' the Mock Turtle replied, counting off the subjects on his flippers, – 'Mystery, ancient and modern, with Seaography: then Drawling – the Drawling-master was an old conger-eel, that used to come once a week: he taught us Drawling, Stretching and Fainting in Coils.'

'What was that like?' said Alice.

'Well, I can't show it you, myself,' the Mock Turtle said, 'I'm too stiff. And the Gryphon never learnt it.'

'Hadn't time,' said the Gryphon: 'I went to the Classical master, though. He was an old crab, he was.'

'I never went to him,' the Mock Turtle said with a sigh. 'He taught Laughing and Grief, they used to say.'

'So he did, so he did,' said the Gryphon, sighing in his turn; and both creatures hid their faces in their paws.

'And how many hours a day did you do lessons?' said Alice, in a hurry to change the subject.

'Ten hours the first day,' said the Mock Turtle: 'nine the next, and so on.'

'What a curious plan!' exclaimed Alice.

'That's the reason they're called lessons,' the Gryphon remarked: 'because they lessen from day to day.'

📖 Glossary

pun a play on words that have different meanings but sound similar or are spelled the same way

homophones words which sound alike but have different meanings

gryphon an imaginary beast with the head and wings of an eagle and the body of a lion

🕐 Extra Time

Find and list some puns used in everyday life. For instance, look at the names of local hairdressers' salons. Explain how the puns work.

5 Under the Skin

↺ Objective

Evaluate the way in which folk tales exploit the theme of outward appearance.

In folk tales, a common **theme** is things not being what they appear to be. From Cinderella to the Frog Prince, a character's appearance doesn't necessarily reflect who they are. The extract that begins on page 70 is taken from the folk tale 'Bearskin', which tells the story of a soldier who makes a pact with the Devil.

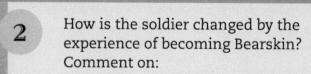

✎ Activities

1 Make a list of the folk tales you know. Discuss how the following themes are presented in these stories:

- identity
- deception
- appearance and reality.

For example, the Fairy Godmother changes Cinderella's appearance so that she can attend the ball, but the Prince is able to discover Cinderella's real identity from the shoe that she leaves behind.

2 How is the soldier changed by the experience of becoming Bearskin? Comment on:

- his physical appearance
- his behaviour and actions
- his thoughts and feelings.

📖 Glossary

theme   subject or main idea

3 Which of the following statements do you think the teller of the story wants readers to agree with? Find evidence from the story to support your answer.

- It's important to be charitable and help others rather than just thinking about yourself.

- You shouldn't judge people by how they look but by the way they act.

- If you endure hard times and adversity you will get your reward in the end.

- You should always keep the promises you make.

4 Folk tales are fast-paced and don't tend to include detailed descriptions. Plan what will happen in the rest of the story and decide how to tell this in the simplest way possible.

5 Using your plan from Activity 4, now write your continuation of the story. Decide:

- what will happen to Bearskin
- what will happen to the youngest daughter
- what will happen to the other two daughters.

SPAG

Try to use a regular subject–verb–object sentence structure and only use adjectives and adverbs where absolutely necessary.

☑ Progress Check

Swap your story with somebody else. Ask them to give the story a rating, on a scale of 1 to 5, with 5 being the highest, on:

- how effectively you have presented the themes

- how satisfying the ending is.

🕐 Extra Time

Read the complete story of 'Bearskin' to see how the original ending compares to yours.

ignite INTERVIEW

'You want to be drawn into a story. You want to be taken on an adventure and that is why nothing is quite how it seems.'

Debbie Korley

More to explore

Extract from 'Bearskin' by the Brothers Grimm

"For the next seven years neither wash thyself, nor comb **thy** beard, nor thy hair, nor cut thy nails, nor say one **paternoster**. I will give thee a coat and a cloak, which during this time **thou** must wear. If thou diest during these seven years, thou art mine; if thou remainest alive, thou art free, and rich to boot, for all the rest of thy life." The soldier thought of the great extremity in which he now found himself, and as he so often had gone to meet death, he resolved to risk it now also, and agreed to the terms. The Devil took off his green coat, gave it to the soldier, and said, "If thou hast this coat on thy back and puttest thy hand into the pocket, thou wilt always find it full of money." Then he pulled the skin off the bear and said, "This shall be thy cloak, and thy bed also, for thereon shalt thou sleep, and in no other bed shalt thou lie, and because of this **apparel** shalt thou be called Bearskin." After this the Devil vanished.

The soldier put the coat on, felt at once in the pocket, and found that the thing was really true. Then he put on the bearskin and went forth into the world, and enjoyed himself, refraining from nothing that did him good and his money harm. During the first year his appearance was passable, but during the second he began to look like a monster. His hair covered nearly the whole of his face, his beard was like a piece of coarse felt, his fingers had claws, and his face was so covered with dirt that if cress had been sown on it, it would have come up. Whosoever saw him, ran away, but as he everywhere gave the poor money to pray that he might not die during the seven years, and as he paid well for everything he still always found shelter. In the fourth year, he entered an inn where the landlord would not receive him, and would not even let him have a place in the stable, because he was afraid the horses would be scared. But as Bearskin thrust his hand into his pocket and pulled out a handful of **ducats**, the host let himself be persuaded and gave him a room in an outhouse. Bearskin was, however, obliged to promise not to let himself be seen, lest the inn should get a bad name.

As Bearskin was sitting alone in the evening, and wishing from the bottom of his heart that the seven years were over, he heard a loud lamenting in a neighbouring room. He had a compassionate heart, so he opened the door, and saw an old man weeping bitterly, and wringing his hands. Bearskin went nearer, but the man sprang to his feet and tried to escape from him. At last when the man perceived that Bearskin's voice was human he let himself be **prevailed on**, and by kind words Bearskin succeeded so far that the old man revealed the cause of his grief. His property had dwindled away by degrees, he and his daughters would have to starve, and he was so poor that he could not pay the innkeeper, and was to be put in prison. "If that is your only trouble," said Bearskin, "I have plenty of money." He caused the innkeeper to be brought **thither**, paid him and put a purse full of gold into the poor old man's pocket besides.

When the old man saw himself set free from all his troubles he did not know how to be grateful enough. "Come with me," said he to Bearskin; "my daughters are all miracles of beauty, choose one of them for thyself as a wife. When she hears what thou hast done for me, she will not refuse thee. Thou dost in truth look a little strange, but she will soon put thee to rights again." This pleased Bearskin well, and he went. When the eldest saw him she was so terribly alarmed at his face that she screamed and ran away. The second stood still and looked at him from head to foot, but then she said, "How can I accept a husband who no longer has a human form? The shaven bear that once was here and passed itself off for a man pleased me far better, for at any rate it wore a **hussar's** dress and white gloves. If it were nothing but ugliness, I might get used to that." The youngest, however, said, "Dear father, that must be a good man to have helped you out of your trouble, so if you have promised him a bride for doing it, your promise must be kept." It was a pity that Bearskin's face was covered with dirt and with hair, for if not they might have seen how delighted he was when he heard these words. He took a ring from his finger, broke it in two, and gave her one half, the other he kept for himself. He wrote his name, however, on her half, and hers on his, and begged her to keep her piece carefully, and then he took his leave and said, "I must still wander about for three years, and if I do not return then, thou art free, for I shall be dead. But pray to God to preserve my life."

📖 Glossary

thy your	**ducats** coins
paternoster prayer	**prevailed on** persuaded
thou you	**thither** there
apparel clothing	**hussar** a soldier

6 Deception and Lies

↺ Objective

Explore the ideas and issues around deception and mistaken identity through discussion and improvisation.

You don't only find the theme of appearance and reality in literature. Have you ever pretended to be older than you really are or wished that you were somebody else? Read the newspaper article on page 73 about Frédéric Bourdin, a 23-year-old Frenchman who managed to convince a family in Texas that he was their missing teenage son.

✎ Activities

1 Discuss why you think Frédéric Bourdin pretended to be Nicholas Barclay. You should:

- consider the reasons why people pretend to be older or younger than they are

- speculate about his possible motives, e.g. he might not have a family of his own, etc.

- explore what type of person the evidence suggests Frédéric Bourdin is.

2 Discuss why you think the Barclay family believed that Frédéric Bourdin was their missing son Nicholas. You should:

- consider how easy or difficult it is to pass as younger or older than you are

- speculate about the possible reasons why the Barclay family accepted Frédéric Bourdin as their missing son

- think about how you and your own family would react in similar circumstances.

3 Improvise a scene where the Barclay family discover that the person they thought was their missing son is actually Frédéric Bourdin. Think about how:

- the Barclay family would react

- what Frédéric Bourdin might say

- voice, silence, stillness and action could be used to suggest their thoughts and emotions.

☑ Progress Check

Perform your scene to the class. Ask them to identify two effective moments in your improvisation and one thing they think you could have improved.

THE CHAMELEON CONMAN

When the family of missing Texan teenager Nicholas Barclay received a phone call saying their son had been found alive, they did not realize they were about to fall victim to the Chameleon. 23-year-old French conman Frédéric Bourdin managed to convince the Barclay family that he was their missing son, even though he was seven years older than Nicholas, his eyes were a different colour, his ears a different shape and he spoke with a French accent.

Bourdin had dyed his brown hair blond and used a pen to fake the same tattoo that Nicholas Barclay wore on his hand. However, to explain the other differences in his appearance, he claimed that he had been kidnapped, taken to Europe and experimented on. For five months he lived with the Barclay family as their son, attending Nicholas Barclay's old school and hanging out with his old friends.

It was only when Charlie Parker, a private investigator hired by a TV company to look into the case, began to raise his suspicions about the true identity of 'Nicholas Barclay' that Frédéric Bourdin's deception started to unravel. Arrested by the FBI, Bourdin was sentenced to six years in prison.

However, this wasn't the first time that Bourdin had pretended to be somebody else. From the age of 16 he had travelled across Europe, using fake identities to con his way into children's homes, schools and hospitals. To appear younger than his real age, Bourdin used hair removal cream, changed his deep voice and even wore a baseball cap to cover his bald patch. He was so successful at taking on these different identities that Interpol dubbed him the Chameleon.

7 Beneath the Disguise

↻ Objective

Develop, through rehearsal and discussion, a personal response to lines from Shakespeare's *Twelfth Night*.

ignite INTERVIEW

'With Shakespeare's plays it is lovely to see why that character made that particular choice at that time – we want to see that person's story.'

Debbie Korley

At first sight, Shakespeare's plays can appear confusing. However, the language and themes are more straightforward and relevant than many people think. One of the common themes of Shakespeare's comedies is disguise and mistaken identity. In Shakespeare's time, this was made more humorous as male actors played the parts of female characters. In the play *Twelfth Night* a female character, Viola, disguises herself as a man and takes the name Cesario. In the extract on page 75, Duke Orsino explains why he wants Cesario to visit the Lady Olivia on his behalf.

✎ Activities

1a Working in pairs, read the extract aloud. One person should read Duke Orsino's words and the other should read Viola's words.

◆ Support

Stand up when reading these words aloud in your pairs. This will help you say the words more clearly and with more emphasis.

1b Swap roles and read the lines aloud again.

2 Discuss what you think is happening in this extract. What do you think Orsino and Viola are saying?

3 In your own words, write brief notes explaining:

- what is happening in this extract
- what you have learned about Orsino and Viola
- what you learn about Viola in her 'Aside' lines.

4 Share your ideas with another pair. How far are your interpretations the same?

5 Rehearse the extract again. This time, try to include more emphasis in your words, varying the intonation, tone and volume of your voice to emphasise words and phrases that you believe are important. You could also try to include some appropriate gestures and facial expressions as well.

Extract from *Twelfth Night* by William Shakespeare

DUKE ORSINO O, then unfold the passion of my love,

Surprise her with **discourse** of my **dear faith**:

It shall become thee well to act my woes;

She will **attend it** better in **thy** youth

Than in a **nuncio's** of more **grave aspect**.

VIOLA I think not so, my lord.

DUKE ORSINO Dear lad, believe it;

For they shall yet **belie** thy happy years,

That say thou art a man: **Diana's** lip

Is not more smooth and **rubious**; thy small **pipe**

Is as the maiden's **organ**, shrill and sound,

And all is **semblative** a woman's part.

I know thy **constellation** is right apt

For this affair.

[…]

VIOLA I'll do my best

To woo your lady:

Aside

Yet, a **barful strife**!

Whoe'er I woo, myself would be his wife.

📖 Glossary

aside (in a play) words spoken to the audience that characters on the stage do not hear

discourse reasoning

dear faith heartfelt love

attend it pay attention to it

thy your

nuncio messenger

grave aspect solemn features

belie contradict

Diana a goddess

rubious ruby-red

pipe voice

organ speech organ, voice

semblative resembling

constellation character or nature

barful strife inner conflict

⑧ Truth and Nonsense

↺ Objective

Develop an understanding of the role of the fool in *Twelfth Night*.

In Shakespeare's time, **fools** and clowns were employed by wealthy nobles to entertain and amuse them. Although a source of comedy, in Shakespeare's plays, it is often the fool who speaks the most sense. This is still true today, an example being Homer Simpson in *The Simpsons*. In the play *Twelfth Night*, Feste is a fool employed by Lady Olivia. Here, he tries to convince Olivia not to fire him by displaying his wit.

📖 Glossary

fool a colourfully-clothed entertainer who was allowed to use humour to criticize his master or mistress in amusing ways

madonna my lady

dexterously skilfully

catechise instruct by asking questions

good my mouse of virtue my good virtuous mouse

bide endure

tabour a small drum

live by earn your living with

doth does

mayst may

cheveril soft leather

Extract from *Twelfth Night* by William Shakespeare

FESTE   Good **madonna**, give me leave to prove you a fool.

OLIVIA   Can you do it?

FESTE   **Dexterously**, good madonna.

OLIVIA   Make your proof.

FESTE   I must **catechise** you for it, madonna: **good my mouse of virtue**, answer me.

OLIVIA   Well, sir, for want of other idleness, I'll **bide** your proof.

FESTE   Good madonna, why mournest thou?

OLIVIA   Good fool, for my brother's death.

FESTE   I think his soul is in hell, madonna.

OLIVIA   I know his soul is in heaven, fool.

FESTE   The more fool, madonna, to mourn for your brother's soul being in heaven. Take away the fool, gentlemen.

✎ Activities

1 What reason does Feste give to prove Olivia is a fool? Explain whether you agree with him.

2 Fools have a licence to speak the truth – no matter who they are talking to. Discuss how this extract shows this.

Now read the extract below. Here, Viola encounters Feste who is playing a **tabour**.

3 Explain what Feste means when he says, 'A sentence is but a cheveril glove to a good wit: how quickly the wrong side may be turned outward!' Pick out quotations that demonstrate this.

4 Make a list of the characteristics of a fool that Feste shows in these extracts. Discuss and rank these in order of importance.

Extract from *Twelfth Night* by William Shakespeare

VIOLA   Save thee, friend, and thy music: dost thou **live by** thy tabour?

FESTE   No, sir, I live by the church.

VIOLA   Art thou a churchman?

FESTE   No such matter, sir: I do live by the church; for I do live at my house, and my house **doth** stand by the church.

VIOLA   So thou **mayst** say, the king lies by a beggar, if a beggar dwell near him; or, the church stands by thy tabour, if thy tabour stand by the church.

FESTE   You have said, sir. To see this age! A sentence is but a **cheveril** glove to a good wit: how quickly the wrong side may be turned outward!

🕐 Extra Time

Find out more about *Twelfth Night*. You could read a graphic novel or watch a film version.

9 Assessment: Reading Analysis of an Extract from *Madame Doubtfire*

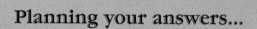

You are now going to read an extract (on pages 80–81) from the novel *Madame Doubtfire* by Anne Fine. In this novel, Daniel and Miranda Hilliard have divorced and their three children, Lydia, Christopher and Natalie, are caught in the middle of their arguments. When Miranda stops Daniel from seeing his children as often as he would like and resolves to hire a nanny to look after them instead, Daniel decides to disguise himself as Madame Doubtfire to apply for the job.

In English exams, for example at GCSE level, you need to be able to analyse literature texts and respond to specific questions. Read the extract on pages 80–81 and then, using the skills you have developed throughout this unit, answer the questions on page 79.

Planning your answers...

Think about the questions as you read the extract. Make notes of any details that you think it might be helpful to refer to when you answer the questions.

Writing your answers...

Remember to use **Standard English** and refer to evidence and quotations from the text.

📖 Glossary

Standard English   the variety of English that is regarded as 'correct' and is used in more formal situations. It is not specific to any geographical area and can be spoken or written.

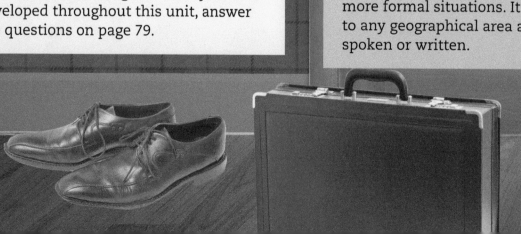

✎ Activities

1 Look again at the opening paragraph. Pick out three details and explain how they suggest that Madame Doubtfire isn't who she claims to be.

2 What impression do you get of Miranda's feelings towards Madame Doubtfire? Comment on the following quotations:

- 'She sat like a fortress at the table, reeking of lavender water, solid and steady and imperturbable.'

- 'Miranda smiled, and felt herself relax.'

- 'On an impulse, Miranda reached out and laid a hand on the bulky sleeve, in order to prevent her from rising.'

3 Knowing what the reader understands about the context of this situation, explain how the themes of deception and disguise create humour in the extract. You should comment on:

- the events of the extract and what the characters' dialogue reveals

- how the themes of deception and disguise are presented.

4 Why do you think Daniel has decided to disguise himself as Madame Doubtfire? Refer to evidence from the extract to explain your answer.

More to explore

Extract from *Madame Doubtfire* by Anne Fine

She took a sideways look at this most unusual job applicant as she poured out the coffee. The woman was huge, even taller than Miranda herself, and large boned with it. Her features were heavy, and scarcely improved by the layer of pancake make-up and streaks of colouring. Miranda could not see her hair, apart from a few dark wisps creeping out from beneath the extraordinary turban. Though her fingernails were beautifully lacquered, her hands were rough, and a little horny. Her feet were enormous. Miranda gauged the wellingtons at size eleven at the very smallest.

You'd think the very sight of the woman would terrify the average child.

And yet... and yet...

There was something terribly reassuring about her. She sat like a fortress at the table, reeking of lavender water, solid and steady and imperturbable.

'Such an attractive way of storing food,' she was saying in her reverberant, soothing manner. 'In those tall glass jars. Worth all the extra trouble, I always think.'

'My husband didn't,' Miranda recalled. 'He hated those jars with a passion. Called them a stupid, fiddly waste of time.'

'Kept spilling, did he? Making his little messes all over the table? Not sure how many beans he could tip in? Not knowing where to store the leftovers?'

Miranda smiled, and felt herself relax. It had been a long day at the Lighting Emporium, and she had been more than a little taken aback to bump into this giantess sailing down her own stairs. But Madame Doubtfire seemed such a nice and understanding lady. And Natalie had slipped off like a sleepy angel, with none of the customary bedtime battles about not wanting to brush her teeth because of the wobbly ones, no pleas for another story, no stalling, no fuss. If only every evening could be as easy. But Natalie was only one of the three. What would the others make of Madame Doubtfire?

'Separated, are you, dear? You and your husband?'

'Divorced.'

'Oh, I'm sorry. Marriage can be a great blessing.'

'Divorce can be even more of one,' answered Miranda.

Madame Doubtfire looked shocked. In order to defend herself,

Miranda added:

'My husband was a very difficult man.'

'Beat you, did he?' suggested Madame Doubtfire. 'Knocked you about a bit, kept you short of housekeeping, frightened the little ones, that kind of thing?'

'Oh, no,' said Miranda. 'Nothing like that. He's not a violent man. Far from it. The children adore him. And insofar as he ever earns any money at all, which isn't very often, he isn't mean.'

There was a silence. Then Madame Doubtfire said:

'If you don't mind my saying so, dear, your ex-husband sounds like quite a bit of a catch.'

Miranda laughed shortly.

'Dead right,' she agreed. 'A real catch. Like the measles.'

At this, Madame Doubtfire began to gather the folds of her salmon-pink coat more closely around her.

'Well, dear,' she said regretfully. 'It's getting on, and I must really think of –'

On an impulse, Miranda reached out and laid a hand on the bulky sleeve, in order to prevent her from rising.

'Oh, please don't go. Please stay and meet the other two children. And then, if you like them...'

Madame Doubtfire was staring at the hand on her arm as if it came from outer space. Miranda was about to withdraw when the great bear fingers came down on hers, and patted them gently.

'You'd like me to consider the job?'

'I would. I really would. You seem quite perfect.'

4

Technology Matters

Do technological advances always benefit us?

Introduction

New technology can bring great changes. Many of these changes are beneficial, but some have damaging consequences.

In this unit, you will explore past, present and possible future technological changes, developing your English skills to research, explain, argue and present your ideas. In the final lessons, you will prepare and present your views about investing in future technologies.

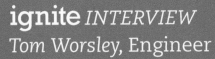

ignite *INTERVIEW*
Tom Worsley, Engineer

What really interests me are the concepts that don't yet exist. If you think about holes in the ozone layer, if you think about global warming, these are largely man-made problems that have come about through technology. Yet because of the constant evolution of technology, we are now designing ways around these problems. What defines good design? A solution looking for a problem is not going to get you anywhere, so you need to be targeted in what you are trying to achieve. It needs to fulfil the purpose for which it has been designed without causing you another problem in doing so.

Activities

1 Choose one item of technology that you could not live without. Explain why it is important to you.

1 Great Innovations

↻ Objective

Make a sustained contribution to group discussion, listening and building on what is said.

New technology transforms the lives of each new generation. You probably can't imagine a world without computers or mobile phones, but some parents and most grandparents lived in such a world.

✎ Activities

1a Look at the technological innovations on this page and page 85. In a group, discuss which one of the innovations you think is the most important. Make sure everyone takes a turn speaking and that others listen carefully. Ask questions to make sure you understand each other's viewpoints.

1b After your discussion, rank the innovations in descending order, with the one that you think is the most important at the top.

1c As a group, agree which one other invention could be added to the list to make the Top 10 Inventions of All Time. Appoint a spokesperson to explain your addition and why you think it is so important.

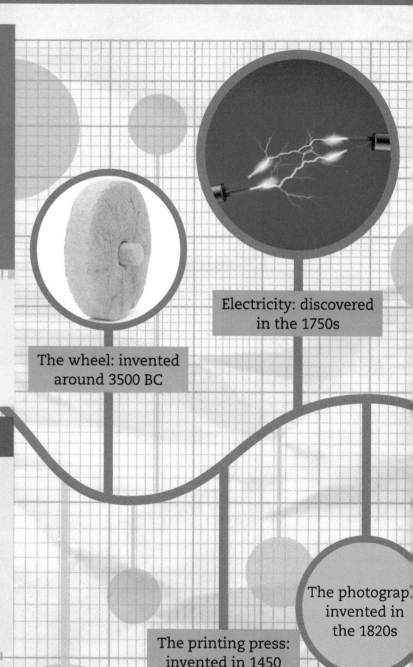

The wheel: invented around 3500 BC

Electricity: discovered in the 1750s

The photograph: invented in the 1820s

The printing press: invented in 1450

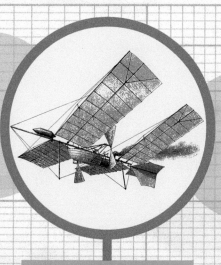

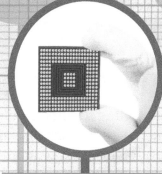

The Internet: invented in the late 20th century

The aircraft: earliest versions invented in the 1880s

The internal combustion engine used by the motor car: invented in the 1860s

The microchip: invented in the 1950s

Antibiotics to treat serious illness: developed in the 1870s

☑ Progress Check

How good are your speaking and listening skills? Give yourself a rating between 1 and 3 (3 being the highest score) in each of the following areas:

- Listening to other people
- Asking relevant questions
- Expressing your viewpoint clearly
- Suggesting new ideas.

🕐 Extra Time

Interview an elderly friend or relative about what they think have been the biggest technological changes in their lifetime. Do they think these developments were a good thing? Did they bring any disadvantages?

② The Price of Progress

↻ Objective

Analyse how descriptive devices convey a strong message to the reader.

In the late 18th and early 19th centuries, new technology had a huge effect on people's lives. The invention of the steam engine and increasing use of coal led to an Industrial Revolution, changing Britain from an agricultural economy to an industrial one. Towns and cities expanded as people moved away from the countryside to find work in factories.

Read the extract from *Hard Times* on page 87. This novel was written by Charles Dickens in 1854 and it describes some of the changes brought about by the Industrial Revolution. The fictional town it describes is called 'Coketown'.

📖 Glossary

metaphor   describing something as something else, not meant to be taken literally, e.g. *You are a star*.

simile   a comparison which uses the words 'like' or 'as', e.g. *The shadowy figure stood as still as a tombstone*.

connotation   the underlying ideas and feelings suggested by a word

✎ Activities

1 If you were to paint a picture of Coketown, which main colours would you use? How would these compare with a countryside scene? What impression does Dickens create through his description of colour?

2 Dickens writes about two animals in this extract, one as a **metaphor** and the other as a **simile**. Explain the effect of these images on our understanding of Coketown.

▨ Support

- Think about the **connotations** of snakes. Are they generally positive or negative?

- What do the words 'in a state of melancholy madness' add to the simile?

3 What sounds does Dickens mention in his description? What do these suggest about life in Coketown?

4 How does Dickens use repetition in the last sentence to reinforce what he is saying? Think about repetition of phrases and structure, as well as individual words.

5 What do you think Dickens felt about the effects of the Industrial Revolution, from his description of Coketown? Write a short paragraph starting: **From his description of Coketown, I think that Dickens felt that…** Use evidence from the text to back up your views.

📖 Glossary

interminable   never ending

monotonously   boringly, without changing

counterpart   something that has the same purpose as another

ignite INTERVIEW

'I would like to go back in time to the Victorian era when all the best inventions were first made. These guys had the biggest ideas and just to be there, in that kind of environment, it would be like going into space today.'

Tom Worsley

Extract from *Hard Times* by Charles Dickens

It was a town of red brick, or of brick that would have been red if the smoke and ashes had allowed it… It was a town of machinery and tall chimneys, out of which **interminable** serpents of smoke trailed themselves for ever and ever, and never got uncoiled. It had a black canal in it, and a river that ran purple with ill-smelling dye, and vast piles of building full of windows where there was a rattling and a trembling all day long, and where the piston of the steam-engine worked **monotonously** up and down, like the head of an elephant in a state of melancholy madness. It contained several large streets all very like one another, and many small streets still more like one another, inhabited by people equally like one another, who all went in and out at the same hours, with the same sound upon the same pavements, to do the same work, and to whom every day was the same as yesterday and tomorrow, and every year the **counterpart** of the last and the next.

9017

3 Selling Technology

↻ Objective

Explore how webpages can relay information concisely and promote new products.

Adlens is a technology business that makes glasses with adjustable lenses. The company combines commercial success with **philanthropy**. Look at the webpages from the Adlens website on pages 90–91.

📖 Glossary

philanthropy   concern for others, shown by kind and generous acts that benefit many people

✎ Activities

1 John Lennon was a singer and songwriter, best known as one of the Beatles, the English rock band formed in the 1960s. Lennon became an icon for his beliefs and style, as well as his music. Why is there an image of him on the first Adlens webpage?

▧ Support

Discuss the possible answers to Activity 1 below. Decide which ones you agree and disagree with and explain why.

There is an image of John Lennon on the first Adlens webpage:

- so that people know what Lennon looked like
- to show what sort of glasses he wore
- because he represents beliefs and values that many people share
- to encourage people to buy glasses from Adlens.

2 What other layout and presentational devices are used on the first webpage to help promote Adlens? Think about the effect of:

- the quotation
- graphics
- headings
- colour
- fonts
- repetition
- symmetry
- hyperlinks.

3 How does the word 'vision' link the glasses with worldwide change?

Now look at the 'Charitable Commitment' webpage on page 91.

4 Who is James Chen and why do you think his quotation is so prominent on this webpage?

5 How does the webpage make use of logos, slogans and statistics? What is their effect?

6 In your own words, summarize how Adlens hopes to use technology to help people in the developing world.

🕑 Extra Time

Find another website promoting a technological product. Explain what layout and presentational devices it uses to create specific effects on the reader.

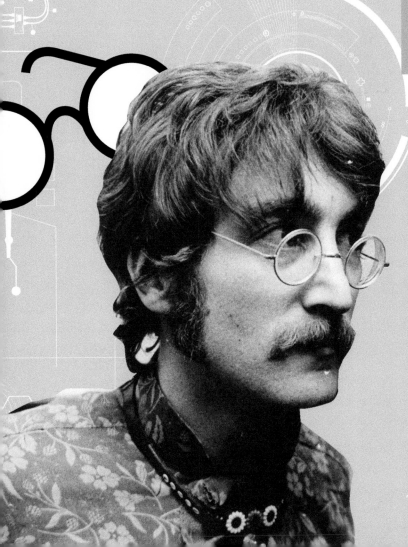

More to explore

Buy a pair   Careers   Media Centre   Eyecare Professionals

Home   Our Glasses   Innovation   About Adlens®   Contact

INSTANT
PRESCRIPTION
EYEWEAR

JOHN LENNON™

John Lennon™ variable focus eyewear

John Lennon's™ iconic look would not be complete without his distinctive round shaped glasses. Inspired by his work, his life and his style, Adlens® has created a new range of variable focus eyewear. Imagine modern technology meets legendary styling with a social conscience.

"Adlens® technology is such an interesting concept with such amazing potential that really captures the imagination. I am sure John would be proud to be associated with the glasses and the ethos behind them."

- Yoko Ono

Instant prescription eyewear

Harness the physical and philosophical essence of John Lennon™. A constant advocate for positive, worldwide change his vision of a better world is echoed in our variable focus lens technology. Adlens® strive to transform the way people see the world. Our life changing Buy One Give One programme is bringing better vision to the whole world, one nation at a time. Join us.

✓ Socially responsible

✓ Empowering those with vision correction needs in less developed countries

✓ Breaking the cycle of deprivation

Tell me more →

Buy a pair

Buy a pair   Careers   Media Centre   Eyecare Professionals

Home   Our Glasses   Innovation   About Adlens®   Contact

Charitable Commitment

Vision for a Nation

Like Adlens®, Vision for a Nation Foundation was founded by James Chen. It aims to provide universal access to eyeglasses.

The Foundation launched its first programme in Rwanda: a country with just 14 eye care professionals to serve a population of more than 10 million people. The Charity's innovative collaboration with Rwanda's Ministry of Health will dramatically improve access to vision correction by empowering the country's burgeoning network of nurses and health workers to provide basic vision assessments and affordable eyeglasses to all who need them.

"That this technology could change lives for the better was obvious...We see endless possibilities for variable focus lens technology. I believe we are just at the beginning of a journey that will transform people's vision around the world."

James Chen

Buy One Give One

Buy One Give One is an innovative programme established by Adlens® designed to contribute towards breaking the cycle of deprivation in less developed countries. For every pair of glasses purchased from The John Lennon™ Collection and Hemisphere® Sun and Optical ranges, Adlens® donates a pair of glasses to someone in the developing world via the Buy One Give One initiative with our charitable partners Vision for a Nation.

Variable focus eyewear reduces the time and ongoing costs associated with traditional eyecare, overcoming fundamental barriers to treatment in countries with fewer resources. 85% of Rwandans live in rural areas - Vision for a Nation trains health care workers to provide immediate and long-term eyecare in their local community.

How it works

4 A Clear Message

↻ Objective

Write clearly and precisely to convey specific detailed information in Standard English.

New inventions and new ideas need careful explanation for them to be understood. If you have a new product to manufacture, you have to write very clear, precise, detailed instructions to make sure it is produced to an exact **specification**.

Read the product specification on page 93. The annotations highlight language features that help to make the specification clear and precise.

📖 Glossary

specification an exact and detailed description of an object or task

Standard English the variety of English that is regarded as 'correct' and is used in more formal situations. It is not specific to any geographical area and can be spoken or written.

ignite INTERVIEW

'Every step along the way I need to be able to write specifications – a technical document that absolutely defines every aspect of what this product is – to make sure that what I get is what I want.'

Tom Worsley

✏️ Activities

1 Think of a new product that you would like to develop, manufacture, market and sell for profit. If you can't think of an idea, choose one of the following products:

- a mobile telephone worn as a wristwatch
- a lipstick with three different shades, all in the same tube
- shoes with variable height heels
- variable size trainers.

2 Write a clear specification for your design team who will develop the product to your requirements. Write in **Standard English** and use the language features highlighted on page 93 to ensure your specification is clear and accurate.

3 Once the product has been developed and manufactured, it needs to be marketed. Write a list of the five most important things your sales team will need to communicate to possible customers about your product.

PRODUCT SPECIFICATION

Product:

A waterproof, shock-resistant case to protect an iPhone when it is being used in extreme conditions.

Adjectives add detail

Subordinate clause explains circumstances for use

Materials:

The case should be manufactured from high-quality polycarbonate moulding. It must provide shock-resistant protection to all phones dropped from up to 3 metres above the ground.

*Use of **passive** to keep the main focus on the product*

Technical detail about material

Statistics give clear guidance

Design features:

- The case must fit tightly around the iPhone to prevent any movement in the event of the phone being dropped.

- Pop-up flaps should be included to cover the input ports for charger, headphones and camera lens. These must be watertight, but should be easy to open when access to the ports is required.

- There should be a large, close-fitting, transparent, soft, thermoplastic cover over the screen. This must be thin enough to enable touch sensitive use of the functions, but strong enough to offer complete protection to the phone when being used in extreme conditions.

Two requirements outlined

- The Apple logo must appear prominently on the reverse of the case.

Colour:

There should be three colours available: black, vivid red and luminous green.

Modal verb emphasizes need

Cost:

The case must be manufactured to a high standard but still be able to retail at under £25.

Maximum cost stated

Glossary

subordinate clause   a clause which is dependent upon a main clause and cannot stand alone as a complete sentence

passive   the version of a verb whereby the main action is done to the subject, rather than by the subject

modal verb   a verb that changes the meaning of other verbs, often expressing a level of certainty, obligation or ability, e.g. *will, would, can, shall, must* and *ought*

Progress Check

Swap the first draft of your specification with a partner.

- Tick places where you think they have made good use of language or presentational features to convey information.

- Suggest two instances where they might be able to improve the precision or clarity of their work, for example by using a more precise word, giving additional detail or including another heading.

5 Disaster!

↻ Objectives

- Collate and develop material for a short presentation.

- Convey a consistent viewpoint and use an appropriate level of formality.

Technology can go wrong – sometimes with disastrous results. Your school is having a 'science and technology week' for students, parents and visitors. Many people are doing presentations about the benefits of science and technology, but you have been asked to prepare a presentation called 'When technology goes wrong', based on the Gulf oil spill in 2010.

✎ Activities

1 Use the resources on pages 96–97 to gather material for your presentation. Remember that you will need to present information in a consistent, accessible way, so that younger students as well as adults can understand it.

Consider:

- what happened on 20 April 2010

- the effect on the environment

- the reaction of the US government and BP

- attitudes to technology

- suggestions for alternative sources of energy.

2 Follow the steps below to prepare your presentation.

3 Rehearse your presentation, remembering to speak slowly and clearly, standing still and making eye contact with your audience. Remember you should speak in Standard English, avoiding colloquialisms and slang.

🕐 **Extra Time**

Do some research of your own to find more information that you can include in your presentation.

1 Make notes on key facts and information that you want to include in your presentation.

2 Group your facts into paragraphs and arrange them into a logical sequence. Start with an introduction and finish with a conclusion summing up what you have said.

3 If you are going to use any visuals in your presentation, decide where and how you will display them.

4 Write out your presentation in full. Although you won't be reading out your presentation, it helps to work through what you are going to say in full sentences.

More to explore

Oil Spill in the Gulf

On the night of 20 April 2010, 41 miles off the coast of Louisiana in the Gulf of Mexico, an offshore oil rig exploded, killing 11 people. Over the three months that followed, oil leaked out of the Maconda well at around 35,000 to 60,000 barrels a day; a total of 4.9 million gallons of oil, making this the biggest offshore oil spill in history.

The Deepwater Horizon rig was leased by the oil company BP, who took on full responsibility for the clean-up operation. BP also agreed to compensate individuals for any losses they may have made and set aside $20 billion for these purposes.

Environmental impact

By the following month, the oil had affected 125 miles of the Louisiana coast and went on to reach the coasts of Florida, Alabama and Mississippi. A Coast Guard Commander stated that although the oil could be cleaned from the surface within months, cleaning it out of marshland would take years.

The affected area is home to over 400 species, including the endangered Kemp's Ridley turtle.

Economic impact

The spill affected many different sectors, including tourism, fishing and of course the oil industry. As such, tens of thousands of families felt the economic repercussions due to job losses. 40% of seafood in the U.S. is provided from the affected area, and the spill therefore put these fisherman out of work. There was an effort to provide work for some of these people containing the spill and cleaning the beaches, but many were forced to file for unemployment benefits.

What has been learned from the disaster?

Research needs to be done into how a leak this big can be stopped if it occurs again. More detailed response strategies must be in place, and further regulation and oversight of offshore drilling should be introduced (as is already the practice in many other countries). However, many people feel that the only real solution to avoiding disasters of this kind is to further the work into clean energy sources.

Extract from BP statement, 'Deepwater Horizon accident and response'

How we responded

We have acted to take responsibility for the clean-up working under the direction of the federal government, to respond swiftly to compensate people affected by the impact of the accident, to look after the health, safety and welfare of the large number of residents and people who helped respond to the spill and to support the economic recovery of the Gulf Coast's tourism and seafood industries impacted by the spill [...]

As of 31 December 2012, we had spent more than $14 billion on our response activities. Throughout, we have sought to work closely with government, local residents, our shareholders, employees, the wider industry and the media.

In addition, we have committed long-term funding for independent research to improve our knowledge of the Gulf of Mexico ecosystem and better understand and mitigate the potential impacts of oil spills in the region and elsewhere.

Robert Dudley, a director of BP, speaking about the Gulf of Mexico oil spill, its aftermath and the future of energy

'I do think solar and wind will provide a lot of energy, and natural gas and oil will have roles far out in the future. The reason oil and gasoline are going to be around for such a long time is the molecule of energy – a bundle of energy in a liquid form of hydrocarbon – is such a powerful little transporter of energy. That's why it's in the tanks of our cars and the ships and the airplanes. The biggest thing I hope happens in our grandchildren's time is that people are much more careful with the efficiency of their energy. People today waste a lot of energy.'

Extract from '10 Clean Energy Statements from Obama's Climate Change Speech'

In June 2013, President Obama gave a speech about the US response to climate change.

'The plan I'm announcing today will help us double again our energy from wind and sun. Today, I'm directing the Interior Department to green-light enough private renewable energy capacity on public plans to power more than 6 million homes by 2020.'

6 Who is Watching You?

↻ Objective

Express a point of view clearly in a formal letter to a newspaper.

Developing technology for hidden cameras and secret listening devices has long been part of the world of spies and double agents. However, nowadays, CCTV surveillance cameras are on almost every street corner in the UK.

✎ Activities

1 Discuss whether you think it is a good or bad idea for ordinary people to be under surveillance. Summarize your viewpoint in a tweet of no more than 140 characters.

2a Read the article on page 99, which focuses on the development of new technology that can gather vast amounts of information about people who communicate digitally.

2b Draft a letter to the editor of the newspaper, giving your views about this issue. Think carefully about:

- an appropriate way to address the editor
- the use of Standard English
- paragraphs to structure your ideas
- a suitable conclusion and sign off.

2c Swap your draft with a partner. Comment on two aspects of the letter that you think are strong and one area that could be improved.

2d Revise your letter in the light of your partner's comments. Proofread your final version to check that your spelling, punctuation and grammar are accurate.

BIG BROTHER SPYWARE CAN EVEN PREDICT FUTURE CRIME

Criminals who pose a threat to national security could be caught before they have even committed an offence with software used to track their online behaviour, it is claimed.

Their future movements can be predicted by 'mining' vast amounts of information from social media websites including Facebook and Twitter.

After a few clicks, a detailed picture of their life, including information about their friends, can be built and used to predict where they might be in future and who with.

Campaigners described it as 'the greatest challenge to civil liberties and digital freedom of our age'.

The 'extreme-scale analytics' programme – called Riot (Rapid Information Overlay Technology) – has been created by Raytheon. The US-based group, the world's fifth largest defence contractor, said the software had not yet been sold to any clients. However, it was shared with the US government as part of a joint research effort in 2010 to help build a national security system capable of analyzing 'trillions of entities' from cyberspace […]

Images posted by users on social networks can contain location details automatically embedded by smartphones. Riot uses this information to reveal where the photographs were taken. It also mines Twitter and Facebook data and sifts GPS information from Foursquare, a mobile phone app used by more than 25 million people to alert their friends of their whereabouts.

Mining from public websites for law enforcement is considered legal in most countries. However, Nick Pickles, of Big Brother Watch, said the technology raised concerns about how data could be collected without being regulated.

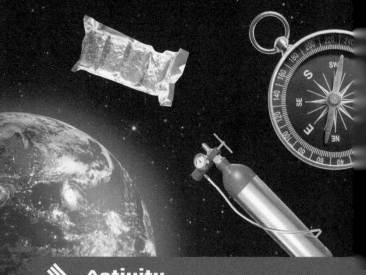

7 Space Challenge

↺ Objective

Participate in a structured group discussion, building on what is said and summarizing the group's conclusions.

Being able to work as part of a team and having good communication skills are essential for any astronaut. The survival task on this page is part of a **NASA** education programme.

📖 Glossary

NASA National Aeronautics and Space Administration, responsible for the US Space programme and aerospace research

Your group is on a space mission to a lunar outpost that has been established on the Moon. Unfortunately, your landing capsule is faulty and lands 80 kilometres away from the outpost. Your survival depends on reaching the outpost, but there is a limit to the resources you can carry.

ignite INTERVIEW

'Communication within a team is extremely important.'

Tom Worsley

✎ Activity

1 Look at the list of equipment available on page 101. As a group, discuss each item in turn and decide how essential it is for your survival. Rank the items in order of importance, with the most important ranked 1, and the least important ranked 15.

Make sure that:

- you read and understand the Moon facts
- you discuss how each item of equipment will be used, as well as ranking its importance
- everyone has an opportunity to give their opinion
- everyone listens carefully
- questions are used constructively and people build on the ideas of others
- each person is responsible for making their own notes about the group's decisions and summarizing their reasons. Everyone should be prepared to represent their group in reporting back to the class.

Moon facts

- There is no atmosphere or liquid on the Moon.
- The lunar soil is loose and includes sharp glassy particles.
- The Moon can be very hot during the day and cold during the night.
- The Moon has no global magnetic field.

space suit repair kit

38 litres of water

map of the Moon's surface

lights powered by solar batteries

thin, light, reflective space blanket

silk parachutes

basic first-aid kit

food concentrate

a handheld mirror for signalling

45kg tanks of oxygen

solar-powered radio receiver-transmitter

15 metres of nylon rope

box of matches

magnetic compass

inflatable life raft

☑ Progress Check

How good were your speaking and listening skills in this challenge? Give yourself a rating between 1 and 3 (3 being the highest score) in each of the following areas:

- Listening to other people
- Explaining your viewpoint clearly
- Suggesting new ideas
- Summarizing the discussion.

🕐 Extra Time

Write the mission's log entries before and after your journey to the outpost.

8 Investing in the future

↻ Objectives

- Structure a presentation to persuade people to support investment in a particular technology.

- Show awareness of other arguments that favour alternative options.

One of the great challenges of the future is how to provide energy for the world's population. You have been invited to present your views to a committee from the Department for Business, Innovation and Skills. They are doing some research to decide which technologies should be given the biggest share of government funding for research and development.

In this lesson, you will be preparing your material for the presentation. In the next lesson, you will be assessed on your presentational skills.

✎ Activities

1 Read about the three main options on pages 103–105: fossil fuels (including the fracking process); renewable resources; and nuclear power. Make sure you look at both the advantages and disadvantages of each.

2 Choose the option that you think should have more investment, so that the technology can be developed further. Do some more research about that option, making notes about why you think it should be pursued rather than the others.

3 Bring all your ideas together and arrange them into a logical sequence of paragraphs. You will need to start with an introduction and finish with a conclusion.

4 Develop your argument into a presentation, deciding what form it will take and which visuals you will use. For example, you might use PowerPoint or just a series of images to accompany your speech.

5 Consider three arguments in favour of other technologies and counter these arguments. Include these counter-arguments in your presentation.

Fossil fuels

Should we invest in technology that will help us to use fossil fuels to supply our future energy needs, for example using fracking?

Advantages

- Fracking (pumping water and chemicals into fissures deep in the Earth's crust in order to release gas and oil) could supply the UK with large amounts of fuel, making us less dependent on foreign oil and gas.

- Fracking leaves the landscape relatively unspoilt, after the extraction.

- Fracking is already used profitably in the US and has helped to lift the country out of recession.

- Some people believe that it causes little damage to the environment.

- Fracking is an established technology, but more investment could make it more efficient and limit possible environmental impacts.

Disadvantages

- Fracking still uses fossil fuels, which in time will run out.

- Some people believe that fracking contaminates water supplies and causes earthquakes.

- Fracking involves pumping lots of chemicals deep into the ground. Not all the chemicals can be removed again and they will not degrade. No one knows the long-term consequences of this.

- Some waste fluid is left to evaporate, contaminating the atmosphere.

- Fracking needs huge amounts of water to be transported to drilling sites, which is costly both in money and in environmental terms.

More to explore

Renewable resources

Should we invest in developing technology that will help us to use the world's renewable resources, such as solar, wind, geothermal and wave power?

Advantages

- The power of renewable sources will never run out.

- These resources cause less damage to ecosystems, so are less damaging to the planet.

- These resources usually create less pollution to the land, air and water than other resources.

- Technology development for renewable energy resources is still relatively young, so may provide a lot more sources of power.

Disadvantages

- The amount of power generated from renewable resources is tiny compared to that of fossil fuels or nuclear power.

- Wind turbines spoil the look of the landscape and damage birds and other wildlife.

- The machinery for renewable resources is costly to install and maintain.

- The supply of renewable energy can be irregular.

Nuclear power

Should we invest in developing technology that will help to improve nuclear power?

Advantages

- A lot of energy is produced using a small quantity of materials.

- Raw materials used are fairly cheap and can last a long time.

- When generated safely, there is no pollution to the atmosphere.

- The UK could be self-sufficient if enough nuclear reactors were built.

Disadvantages

- Nuclear reactors are expensive to build and run.

- Leaking of radioactive materials can devastate the surrounding environment for a long time.

- Nuclear waste is toxic and remains toxic for thousands of years.

- The idea of nuclear power is generally unpopular.

9 Assessment: Presenting Your Argument

It is now time to present your views about investing in technology to the committee from the Department for Business, Innovation and Skills.

Yours will be just one among many presentations, so you must try to deliver a convincing argument for backing your chosen technology for investment.

You will need to:

- deliver your pitch with confidence and enthusiasm

- back up what you say with visuals

- answer questions.

Note that you are being tested on your spoken English skills, rather than your writing skills in this assessment.

Before you present...

Remember that an effective presentation will need to:

- have a clear structure which moves from an introduction, through a series of points, and finishes with a conclusion

- have visuals that back up what you say

- be in Standard English, without colloquialisms or slang

- be rehearsed, so that you are not simply reading out what you have written.

You may wish to prepare some outline notes that you can glance at from time to time.

During and after the presentation...

- Speak slowly and clearly, using a variety of vocabulary to express what you have to say.

- Keep the audience interested by varying the pace, intonation and volume of what you say.

- Stand still and try not to fidget. Keep focused on your presentation and audience.

- Maintain eye contact with the audience, and avoid just reading your notes or facing the screen and reading.

- Listen carefully to any questions and think before you respond to them.

5

CAMPAIGN FOR A CAUSE

'Education is the only solution. Education First.'

Oxfam
Thank you
for your support

How can you make someone care about a cause?

Introduction

Would you like to make a difference to the lives of others? Every day, around the world, there are victims of injustice, cruelty and poverty. Charity workers campaign to bring about change to make the world a better place. They do this by building public awareness, raising funds and persuading people to take direct action.

In this unit, you will find out what it's like to work for a charity. You will choose a cause that you feel passionate about and persuade others to take action.

ignite *INTERVIEW*

Kate Geary and Matthew Grainger,
Media and communications at Oxfam

At Oxfam we aim to help improve the lives of poor people. We also lobby the government to change policies, so that when people do rebuild their lives, their lives are built back better than before. The things that you learn in school about writing are exactly the kind of things that matter when you are writing in jobs like ours. The editing process is so important, because if you don't get things right, that is what people remember. What makes for an effective campaign? First and foremost you need a clear message to communicate. Then to be able to communicate for Oxfam why that matters: simplifying the message, communicating really powerfully why that matters and then telling people in a simple direct way, you can do something about this and this is how.

✎ Activities

1 List as many charities as you can. They can be large or small.

2 Share your ideas and group the charities according to the type of cause that they campaign for (e.g. animal rights, environmental issues).

↔ Stretch

Rank the groupings twice:

- first according to which you think the general public are most likely to support
- then according to which you feel are the most important to support.

1 Charity Roles

↻ Objective

Understand the roles and skills of people working for charities.

✎ Activities

1 Many charities rely on volunteers who give time and effort to support a cause. Talk about some charity volunteering you have done or would like to do. This might involve raising money through sponsorship or helping at a local or school fundraising event.

2 Why do you think many people volunteer, even though they don't get paid for their time and efforts?

One of the most well-known charities in the UK is Oxfam. Oxfam campaigns for the rights of people who are suffering injustice around the world. It also works to tackle global poverty through development projects designed to have a lasting impact upon people's lives.

Oxfam gets its funding from the government, private contributions and its retail business – a chain of shops selling donated books, clothes, household items and **Fairtrade goods**.

📖 Glossary

Fairtrade goods   things produced by people paid a fair wage for their work in decent working conditions

As well as relying on the time and effort given by volunteers, charities such as Oxfam also employ people. Some charity jobs are listed below.

- Advocacy officer – the person who advocates (or communicates) issues that the charity works for, including writing reports and lobbying influential people
- Media officer
- Researcher
- E-commerce officer
- Education officer
- Fundraiser.

3 Discuss what you think people in each of the above jobs do. If you're not sure, think about the clues the job title gives you. The first one has been done for you.

4 What skills do you think people need to do each of these jobs?

Support

Think about skills such as reading, writing, communicating with people of different ages and backgrounds, business sense.

5 Which one of these jobs appeals to you most? Why?

Extra Time

Write a job advertisement for one of the charity roles on the left. You could use the outline below to structure your advertisement.

Could you make a difference?

We're an international charity looking for the right person to fill the crucial role of
_____

What will the role entail?

This is your chance to _____

What skills are required?

You will need most, if not all, of the following skills:

- _____
- _____
- _____

If this sounds like you and you genuinely feel as passionate about our cause as we do, please visit our website for an application pack and further details.

JAMES MILLER

FAIRTRADE

2 Agreeing a Cause

↺ Objectives

- Make relevant contributions to discussion, supporting others' contributions.

- Reach an agreement through discussion.

There is a range of causes that a charity might campaign for and support. These causes could be local, national (affecting people in one country) or international (affecting people in many different countries).

✎ Activities

1a Create a three-column grid with the headings 'local causes', 'national causes' and 'international causes'. Add each of the causes listed on the right to the grid, according to whether you think they affect people locally, nationally or internationally.

ignite INTERVIEW

'What makes for an effective campaign? Simplifying the message, communicating really powerfully why that matters and then telling people in a simple direct way, you can do something about this and this is how.'

Kate Geary

A A developing country is hit by famine and, unless the people living there are given aid, many thousands could starve and die.

B £10,000 is needed to build a skate park for teenagers to use in your local area.

C Research is needed into a disease called malaria, which claims millions of victims every year, especially in developing countries.

D Volunteers are needed to provide company for thousands of elderly people in the UK who are housebound, leading them to feel lonely and isolated.

E Some products still use animal testing to check they are safe for humans to use. This can cause pain and suffering to the animals.

F £30,000 is needed for an operation that could help a boy who lives in your town to walk.

1b Add other examples of local, national or international causes of your own to your grid.

1c Choose the top five causes that you think are most important to support. Rank them 1–5, with your favourite as number 1.

1d Make notes about your favourite, explaining why you feel it is important.

Following on from your work above, you are now part of a charity committee. You have been invited to meet with colleagues to decide which cause to support and to agree on a campaign. Here's the **agenda** for the meeting:

Agenda for Meeting of Charity Committee

1 Which cause most deserves our support?

2 What should be our key message to ensure that other people support the cause too?

3 At whom should our message be aimed?

4 What action could people take to support our cause or improve the situation?

5 Any other business.

📖 Glossary

agenda list of things to be discussed or done

2 Create a spider diagram showing the speaking and listening skills you will need to make sure you have a fair and effective meeting. (For example, listen carefully to others and don't interrupt.)

3 In groups, decide who will be:

- Chairperson: who controls the meeting, introducing the topics for discussion and making sure everyone is involved

- Time-keeper: who sets a time limit for each point for discussion and reminds the team if they run over time

- Minute-taker: who notes what is said and what action is agreed

- Summarizer: who explains to the class which charity has been chosen and why.

4 Conduct your meeting, covering the topics on your agenda and reaching an agreement, by vote if necessary.

☑ Progress Check

How effective was your contribution to the group discussion? Give your own performance in each of the skills noted on your spider diagram a mark out of 3 (with 3 being the highest). Set yourself a target to improve your performance in future group discussions.

3 Learning to Listen

↻ Objectives

- Use listening and questioning skills to research and develop material.

- Write a case study.

A charity researcher may be asked to help create case studies, which are often included in campaign material to support a cause. A case study tells the story of an individual linked with the campaign issue. It often includes **direct speech**, as in the following example about a boy living in Liberia who was pressurized into becoming a child soldier.

James's story

'It first happened in 1991,' says James. 'That's when the rebels came to our village in Lofa County in Liberia. They beat my father and put him in jail. Then they asked me if I would join them… I said yes, because I wanted to protect my father because I was sure they were going to kill him. I was six years old. Then they sent us to fight at the front lines. I did that for the next five years… There is nothing more bad than war.'

James stopped being a soldier after five years of fighting in the bush. He is now 18 years old. He has been going to school since he left the front lines. 'I've been asked to fight again, but I've refused. My education is too important to me and I still have a lot to learn in life. If I am educated, I will have a better future, much better than my past.'

Interview conducted on 20 May 2003, Monrovia, Liberia

✎ Activities

1a In your own words, sum up the message that you think Oxfam is trying to communicate through James's story.

1b How do you think readers might react to this case study?

2 In what ways does using direct speech, rather than **reported speech**, make the case study more powerful and persuasive?

📖 Glossary

direct speech   words, within inverted commas in a sentence, actually spoken by someone

reported speech   text that explains what someone said, without necessarily using their exact words

infrastructure   basic public systems, e.g. transport, communication, electricity, water

3 When you interview people for case studies, listening skills are very important. List as many ways as you can that show someone is actively listening, e.g. *Keep constant eye contact.*

4a Write a case study for your chosen cause, or use the cause outlined in the fact file on the right if you prefer. First, think of a person you could interview for your case study.

4b Write five questions you would ask in order to find out how the issue affects this person's daily life.

4c Work with a partner. One of you should be the interviewer and the other should be the interviewee. Ask and answer the questions in character. Use the information in the fact file to help you, if you wish.

4d Listen and make notes on your interviewee's answers (or your own answers if you were the interviewee). Write them up in the form of a case study like James's on page 114.

Fact File

In Liberia, Africa, Oxfam is working to help more of the population become self-sufficient by helping farmers irrigate (control water for) their land.

- After years of civil war in Liberia, much of the **infrastructure** for providing clean water and reducing the risk of flooding was destroyed.

- Lowland farms previously used to grow crops flooded. Upland fields used instead had pest problems and unreliable rainfall.

- Some people became undernourished.

- Farmers, many of whom are women, had to walk long distances to find land suitable for growing. One woman had to walk six miles to farm land to grow rice, meaning that she spent long periods of time away from her children.

- Some children could not go to school, because farmers could not afford fees, uniforms or materials.

4 Getting Your Facts Straight

↻ Objective

Identify reliable factual information from a range of sources.

As part of your campaign, you need to do plenty of research about the issue you are focusing on, to ensure that the information you gather is trustworthy and reliable. You need to collect reliable facts and statistics, and present them clearly without misleading people with opinions and misconceptions, however popular they may be.

✎ Activities

1a List the skills that you think you need to be an effective researcher.

1b For each one, give an example of a time when you have shown that you have this skill. (For example, you might think it is important to ask key questions even if they are unpopular. When have you done this in order to get to the truth?)

2 Not all information should be trusted. For each type of source you could use during your research, make notes on its advantages and disadvantages. Complete a grid like the one started below, adding more sources if you wish.

Source of information	Advantages	Disadvantages
Website	Immediate access, including from mobile devices. Huge range and amount of online information. Current and up-to-date.	Reliability needs to be questioned. The origin of the information isn't always clear.
Reference book		
Talking to people		
Social networking sites		
Government leaflets		
News articles on TV or radio		
Blogs, diaries and letters		

↔ Stretch

What or who else would you use to make your research more reliable and persuasive?

3 When doing research, you need to avoid bias or opinion (unless you acknowledge what they are). Write a brief definition of each of these terms, to remind yourself of how to identify them. Give an example of each. Check your definitions in a dictionary.

When researching the issue that you wish to campaign about, you need to ask yourself questions, like the ones below.

- Who is affected by this cause or issue?
- How does it impact upon these people's daily lives?
- What can be done to help them?
- Who should you **lobby** to make a change?

4 Add more questions that are relevant to your particular issue. Then start your research.

5 Keep a record of your findings in a way that is most helpful to you. Some people like to write lists or record things as mind maps. Other people use Venn diagrams to show how information can overlap or prefer to record things as audio notes.

📖 Glossary

lobby   try to persuade an MP or another official person to support your cause

☑ Progress Check

- Summarize the most important facts that you have discovered during your research in no more than 40 words.

- Ask your partner to check your work, highlighting anything that sounds more like an opinion or biased information than a clear fact.

5 Reporting on a Cause

↺ Objectives

- Explore how meaning is constructed in a formal report.

- Understand how to use adverbials.

A charity's advocacy officer may produce a report for the charity board to explain why a cause is deserving of time and hard-earned funding.

✎ Activities

1 What do you already know about writing reports? Write your ideas on a mind map, including what you know about how to set out a report, how to start and end it, and the sort of language you should use.

2 Read the report written by an advocacy officer on page 119. How has it been organized to make its points clear and easy to follow?

📖 Glossary

adverbial a word or phrase that modifies a verb or clause. They include adverbs but also other types of words and phrases, such as prepositional phrases and subordinate clauses, e.g. *He ran until he was tired.* (subordinate clause as adverbial)

3 Identify four examples in the report where the author uses **adverbials** and explain how they add extra information to the verbs or clauses in the text. For example: *'Every year, millions of animals are subjected to testing.'*

SPAG

The adverbial 'Every year' shows that the problem is a long-standing and ongoing one, suggesting that action is a necessity.

4 As an advocacy officer, write a report to present a case for supporting your chosen cause. Think carefully about:

- the structure of your report

SPAG

- a suitable tone and style of writing

- use of adverbials to convey detail.

Report by advocacy officer about why we should campaign against animal testing

Introduction

Around the world, thousands of animals die every day in experiments to test the safety of a variety of products from medicine to paint. The animals include mice, monkeys, dogs and rabbits. This report is intended to make recommendations on how and why this terrible and unnecessary cruelty must be stopped immediately.

The animal cost

Every year, millions of animals are subjected to testing. In the UK alone over 4 million procedures were carried out on animals during 2012. Many argue that this is unnecessary, given improvements in technology that allow increasingly accurate computerized models to replace experiments on live animals. When testing on a living creature is essential, there are often humans who volunteer to be tested on.

Case study

Take a Golden Retriever called Dog 9 (animals used for experiments often aren't dignified with a name). She was bred in captivity to be tested upon and has never known what it's like to roam freely and enjoy life. Instead, she is locked inside a cage for hours on end, never enjoys the companionship of other animals or people, and is forced to endure intrusive and invasive procedures.

The cost of the cause

There is no doubt that this cause deserves our full energies and support. I estimate that, given the need to use the national media, we will have to dedicate approximately 10% of our current funding to this cause.

Recommendations

In order to stop this cruel and unnecessary practice, we need to take action now. This includes:

- lobbying the UK government to make all animal testing illegal and find a humane alternative

- writing to companies that stock products tested on animals to ask them to stop stocking them

- helping to fund further advances in computerized models that could replace the need to test on any living creature

- raising public awareness through newspaper and online campaigns, so that the demand for these products is reduced.

6 The Press Release

↻ Objective

Understand how structural, presentational and language devices create effects.

One of the key roles of a media officer is to write press releases. A press release gives clear information about a topical or newsworthy event and is aimed at news editors or journalists, rather than the general public. Many journalists and editors use press releases as the basis for writing articles that are then published in magazines, in newspapers or on websites, or as the basis for live news or documentary programmes on TV or radio.

✎ Activities

1a Read the Oxfam press release on page 121 about the chocolate companies Mars, Mondelez and Nestlé. Why do you think the media officer started the press release with an image, and with this particular image?

1b Why do you think some of the text is presented in bold font?

1c Why do you think the media officer refers to Oxfam in the **third person**? **SPAG**

1d Media officers try to use the **active voice** rather than the **passive voice** in their press releases. Find an example of this and explain why the active voice has more impact for the reader.

1e Why do you think the main part of the press release ends with a quotation?

1f How do you think editors and journalists might use the extra information given at the end of the press release?

📖 Glossary

third person referring to organizations or people by name or with the pronouns 'he', 'she', 'it' or 'they' (in contrast to using the first person 'I' or 'we')

active voice in a sentence with an active voice, the subject is doing the action, e.g. *The company employs women.*

passive voice in a sentence with a passive voice, the subject is being acted upon, e.g. *The women are employed by the company.*

Mars, Mondelez, Nestlé are leaving women farmers behind

Oxfam campaigns at chocolate company headquarters on International Women's Day

An investigation into four countries where Mars, Mondelez and Nestlé purchase cocoa has shown that many women farmers face discrimination, unequal pay and hunger, leaving the companies' social policies exposed as weak and needing work, says international agency Oxfam.

Many women farmers in southwest Nigeria cultivate cocoa beans used by major global food companies

'The women who help produce the chocolate we all love to eat are getting left behind.'

Alison Woodhead
Oxfam's Behind the Brands Campaign Manager

Oxfam campaigned today at company headquarters and retail locations on International Women's Day to urge them to address gender inequality in their supply chains. The three companies control 40 percent of the chocolate market and purchase one third of all cocoa, which is mostly grown by small farmers in developing countries. Oxfam's research shows that Mars, Mondelez and Nestlé are doing very little to address poor conditions faced by the women who grow cocoa.

Oxfam's investigation into cocoa supply chains in Brazil, Indonesia, Nigeria and Ivory Coast revealed that:

- **Women cocoa growers are often paid less** than men.

- Most people who work along the cocoa supply chain **continue to live in poverty.**

- Women working in cocoa fields and processing plants suffer substantial **discrimination and inequality.**

- **While women increasingly occupy positions of power** in food and beverage company headquarters, women working in company supply chains in developing countries continue to be denied similar advances in wealth, status or opportunity.

Although the companies do not control or employ them directly, Oxfam is calling on Mars, Mondelez

and Nestlé to lead an aggressive effort to support and protect the rights of the millions of women worldwide who grow the cocoa essential for their products.

Oxfam has given companies a long list of specific steps that can meet recommended goals, including increasing training for women, promoting female recruitment and leadership of farming cooperatives and requiring that suppliers provide a living wage to workers.

'**Rooting out gender inequality** is among the most important things companies can do to improve the quality and sustainability of their products,' said Woodhead. 'Companies see farmers choosing other careers or crops and know how difficult it will be to meet the growing demand for cocoa if the situation does not improve. We are showing companies that consumers will reward them for doing the right thing, and will hold them accountable if they don't.'

Notes to Editors:

- Media briefing: Gender and cocoa (PDF)

- Video: The truth about women and chocolate

- Pictures from the Ivory Coast and Nigeria

Contact Information: Ben Grossman-Cohen, Oxfam Press Officer

More to explore

✎ Activities continued

2 Based on your analysis of the example press release, what features might you expect to find in any press release? List the features under the following headings:

- Structural (how the text is set out and organized)

- Presentational (how different styles, fonts or images are used)

- Language.

📚 Support

Copy these features of a press release under the correct heading: Structural, Presentational or Language.

- A short and clear title

- Organized into paragraphs of related ideas

- Quotations from people or companies involved

- Formal language

- Refers to the charity itself in the third person

- Bullet points used for key information

- Includes statistics

- Written in the active voice

- Ends with a list of actions required

- Relevant image, with caption

3 Now apply what you've learned to writing a press release of your own for the cause that you have chosen. Remember to think carefully about the structure, presentation and language.

You may find it helpful to read through the template provided by Oxfam for a possible press release on page 123.

ignite INTERVIEW

'The editing process is so important, because if you don't get things right, that is what people remember. The other thing is simplicity. It takes skill to write a very, very simple story.'

Matthew Grainger

Oxfam press release template

Heading

The heading should be typed in bold and centred.
Keep it short, snappy and to the point.

Subheading
This is optional and is used to elaborate on the information in the heading.
Again, keep it simple!

First paragraph. Start with a bang. Get the five 'W's in straight away – Who, When, What, Where, Why.

Following paragraphs. Make your points in order of importance. The second paragraph should elaborate on the first. You are essentially telling a story, so you must give the reader the full picture. Spell out the facts, give statistics, and quote names and numbers of people involved.

Quotes. Include a direct quote from the most relevant person involved: it will humanise the story. Keep the quote brief, providing an overview of the event. If writing a quote for somebody else, get their approval before using it. Remember to give the person's full name and job title.

ENDS

This marks the end of your press release. Below, under the 'Contacts' and 'Notes' headings, further information can be found.

FOR MORE INFORMATION PLEASE CONTACT:

Give names, email addresses and telephone numbers of people a journalist can contact for further information.

NOTES TO EDITOR:

This is your last chance to give journalists background information, and links to photographs, websites, etc.

⏱ Extra Time

Try to find examples of other press releases, possibly by searching on the Internet. How do they differ from the Oxfam press release?

7 Into the News

↺ Objective

Compare structural, presentational and language features.

✎ Activities

1 Read the extract from a news article on page 125, which appeared in the Professional section of *The Guardian*. The article is on the same topic as the Oxfam press release on page 121. If there are any unfamiliar words, try to work out their meaning using the context and thinking of any similar words. Then use a dictionary to check.

2 Compare the two texts (on page 121 and 125), using a Venn diagram to show their similarities and differences. Consider:

- purpose
- audience
- content
- whose thoughts and ideas are included
- whether there's any evidence of bias
- how the charity, Oxfam, is presented
- how the text is structured and organized
- the style of the language.

3 How effective do you think this article is in persuading people to support the need for gender equality in cocoa production? Rate it on a scale of 1 to 3, with 3 being the most persuasive. Give reasons for your answer.

4 Plan a short news article about your chosen cause, using the press release you wrote for Activity 3, page 122.

THE GUARDIAN   OXFAM PRESS RELEASE

BOTH!

🕐 Extra Time

Write your news article in full, researching a suitable image and including a caption.

WOMEN IN COCOA PRODUCTION: WHERE IS THE GENDER EQUITY?

Chocolate companies often ignore the important role of women in quality cocoa production but this must change.

Chocolate manufacturers are becoming ever more concerned about the future of cocoa production but have they considered the importance of the gender dimension?

Women sorting out cocoa fruits in a plantation in Indonesia

Women's role in ensuring quality in cocoa production is rarely acknowledged. Supporting women cocoa farmers and workers could deliver enhanced productivity and sustainability in cocoa production, as well as women's economic and social empowerment.

Women in the cocoa-chocolate value chain

Chocolate companies recognise the importance of gender at the consumer end of the cocoa-chocolate value chain. 'A large proportion of boxed chocolates are bought by women for women,' said Jill McCall, brand manager at Kraft Foods.

There is less recognition of women's participation at the production end of the cocoa-chocolate value chain, with cocoa largely deemed as a 'male crop' in Ghana and India. Yet research in both countries has found women often play a role as farmers (an estimated 25% in Ghana), unpaid family labour and/or low-wage casual labour.

Yet in both Ghana and India, there is limited recognition of women's contribution to quality production. They normally receive lower incomes than men, with many below the local minimum wage.

Strategies to promote gender equity

Some within the sector are beginning to wake up to the important role women play in cocoa production. For example: the Fairtrade co-operative Kuapa Kokoo in Ghana has had a gender programme in place since the late 1990s; the Cocoa Partnership, established by Cadbury in 2008, has included a gender focus when supporting local cocoa-growing communities.

In February, Oxfam International launched its Behind the Brands scorecard. This assesses leading food companies based on their own publicly reported activity on issues including gender discrimination.

Many younger cocoa farmers and workers are moving out of agriculture, which means chocolate companies seeking to enhance productivity and quality cocoa urgently need to support women in cocoa production if they are to ensure long-term future cocoa sourcing.

What needs to be done?

Strategies to enhance women's participation, recognition and remuneration in cocoa production, should include:

- recognising women as farmers, in their own right
- providing training and education that are focused on enhancing women's participation and learning
- supporting women's organisations
- supporting implementation of legislation promoting women's equal access to land ownership and remuneration.

Promoting gender equity is an issue that concerns all actors along the cocoa–chocolate value chain (consumers, manufacturers, processors, producers) as well as related governments and organisations. Those chocolate companies that seek quality output but ignore the gender dimension of cocoa sourcing do so at their long-term peril.

8 Fundraising Appeals

↻ Objective

Explore various persuasive devices used in fundraising appeals.

The role of a fundraiser in a charity is to raise money to help the charity achieve its aims.

✎ Activities

1 Read the advertisement on page 127 that the fundraiser for the charity Kitting Out Kids has placed in a local newspaper. Complete a grid like the one started below, identifying the persuasive devices it uses and their effects.

Persuasive technique	What this means	Example from the advertisement	How this might persuade the reader to donate money or time
Rhetorical question	A question asked for effect that doesn't require an answer.	'Will you help us to make a difference?'	This question plays upon the reader's sympathy and conscience.
Emotive language			
	Repeated sound patterns.		
Direct appeal	Using the second-person pronoun 'you' to direct the message to the reader.		
Statistics			
Quotations	Words spoken or written by another person relevant to the campaign.		

2 What presentational devices help to make the texts persuasive? Think about the use of images, captions, different font sizes and colours.

3 As a fundraiser you have been given a small budget to publish an appeal in a local newspaper in order to raise money for your chosen charity. Draft an appeal, using persuasive devices to urge your readers to donate or help.

☑ Progress Check

Swap the draft of your charity advertisement with a partner's. Rate how persuasive your partner's advertisement is on a scale of 1 to 5, with 5 being the most persuasive. Give reasons for your choice and offer advice to your partner about how to make it even more persuasive.

Little Stephen needs your help!

This is Stephen.

He is two years old.

Stephen is a loved and cherished little boy.

The problem is that his family have fallen on hard times.

Like many people throughout our city his mummy and daddy were made redundant and are struggling to find work. As a result, money is tight and the family have to prioritise food over clothing. Winter is approaching and Stephen needs a warm coat and a new pair of shoes – the ones he's wearing at the moment have holes in the bottom and let the rain in. Without these essential items Stephen will be left shivering. This is where Kitting Out Kids come in and where you could too.

Here's what you could do to help:

- Donating just £10 would buy a warm winter coat for a child like Stephen.
- Donating £20 would help us to put shoes on his tiny toes too.
- Volunteering to collect donated clothing or to work at our collection depot.

Just think. One day it could be your friend, child or grandchild in need. Don't turn away, do something to help, today. 'Thanks to Kitting Out Kids my boy now has a coat to keep him warm and was thrilled to build his first snowman.' Mrs A, mummy to three-year-old William. I hope you feel you can support our work and put a smile back on little Stephen's face.

Who are Kitting Out Kids and how do we help?

Kitting Out Kids was set up in 1987 to help families like Stephen's in and around our city. A team of dedicated volunteers collect donations of good quality clothes and pass them on to families who need a helping hand. We also collect your generous cash donations and use them to buy children essential clothing. So far, we have helped more than 3,000 children be warm, play and smile again.

Will you help us to make a difference?

We estimate that there are more than 1,000 families in our city who urgently need our help now.

Kitting Out **Kids**

9 Lobbying for Change

 Objective

Consider the range and overall effect of rhetorical features.

As well as releasing campaign materials to the general public, organizations such as Oxfam also lobby key players in order to encourage them to act. Lobbying can take many different forms, from applying direct pressure through staging a protest or a march to encouraging members of the public to sign an online petition for change.

ignite INTERVIEW

'Lobbying is trying to influence people to do things that they might not necessarily want to do. So, for example, asking them to stop doing things that harm poor people and to do more of the kind of things that actually benefit poor people, such as giving more aid.'

Kate Geary

Activities

1 List the possible advantages and disadvantages of each form of lobbying. Add other examples of the types of action people could take.

Form of lobbying	Possible advantages	Possible disadvantages
Staging a protest		
Signing an online petition		
Vetoing the goods or services of a company or organization		
Making a speech to a key player		

Making a speech can have great impact, particularly if you have an influential audience or it is covered by the media.

When she was 15, Pakistani schoolgirl Malala Yousafzai was shot by Taliban gunmen on her way to school in October 2012. The reason? She dared to defy the law prohibiting girls from having an education. Since recovering from the physical effects of her ordeal, Malala has moved to Britain and continues to campaign for the right of females everywhere to an education.

2a Read the extract on pages 130–131, which is taken from a speech Malala delivered to the United Nations on her 16th birthday. Who are the people Malala wishes to influence through her speech?

2b What is the key message she is communicating? Sum it up in 20 words or fewer.

2c Malala uses a number of contrasts in the opening paragraph. For instance, 'out of silence, came a thousand voices'. How do these add to Malala's message?

2d Malala starts a number of sentences with 'we call'. Why do you think she repeats this opening? To whom might the pronoun 'we' refer?

2e Why do you think that Malala chose to end her speech as she does?

3 You have been invited to deliver a two-minute speech, lobbying a key player to support your cause and take action to make a positive difference. Write the speech.

Start your planning by considering these key questions:

- Who are the people you wish to influence?

- What is the key message you wish to communicate?

- What do you want your audience to do to help the cause?

📑 Support

To add impact to your speech, you might like to include repetition or rhetorical questions (questions asked for effect that don't require an answer).

More to explore

Malala Yousafzai's speech to the United Nations

Dear Friends, on the 9th of October 2012, the Taliban shot me on the left side of my forehead. They shot my friends too. They thought that the bullets would silence us. But they failed. And then, out of that silence, came thousands of voices. The terrorists thought that they would change our aims and stop our ambitions but nothing changed in my life except this: Weakness, fear and hopelessness died. Strength, power and courage was born. I am the same Malala. My ambitions are the same. My hopes are the same. My dreams are the same...

Dear fellows, today I am focusing on women's rights and girls' education because they are suffering the most. There was a time when women social activists asked men to stand up for their rights. But, this time, we will do it by ourselves. I am not telling men to step away from speaking for women's rights rather I am focusing on women to be independent to fight for themselves.

Dear sisters and brothers, now it's time to speak up.

So today, we call upon the world leaders to change their strategic policies in favour of peace and prosperity.

We call upon the world leaders that all the peace deals must protect women and children's rights. A deal that goes against the dignity of women and their rights is unacceptable.

We call upon all governments to ensure free compulsory education for every child all over the world.

We call upon all governments to fight against terrorism and violence, to protect children from brutality and harm.

We call upon the developed nations to support the expansion of educational opportunities for girls in the developing world.

We call upon all communities to be tolerant – to reject prejudice based on cast, creed, sect, religion or gender. To ensure freedom and equality for women so that they can flourish. We cannot all succeed when half of us are held back. We call upon our sisters around the world to be brave – to embrace the strength within themselves and realise their full potential.

Dear brothers and sisters, we want schools and education for every child's bright future. We will continue our journey to our destination of peace and education for everyone. No one can stop us. We will speak for our rights and we will bring change through our voice. We must believe in the power and the strength of our words. Our words can change the world.

Because we are all together, united for the cause of education. And if we want to achieve our goal, then let us empower ourselves with the weapon of knowledge and let us shield ourselves with unity and togetherness.

Dear brothers and sisters, we must not forget that millions of people are suffering from poverty, injustice and ignorance. We must not forget that millions of children are out of schools. We must not forget that our sisters and brothers are waiting for a bright peaceful future.

So let us wage a global struggle against illiteracy, poverty and terrorism and let us pick up our books and pens. They are our most powerful weapons.

One child, one teacher, one pen and one book can change the world.

Education is the only solution. Education First.

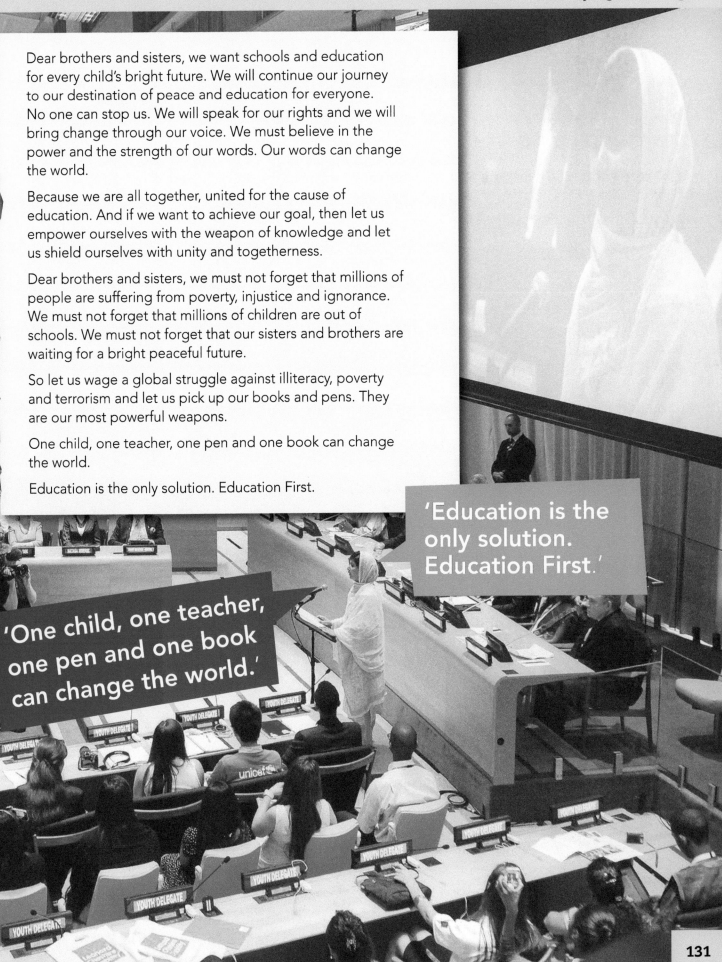

'Education is the only solution. Education First.'

'One child, one teacher, one pen and one book can change the world.'

10 Assessment: Lobbying for Your Cause

Research, plan, write and edit.

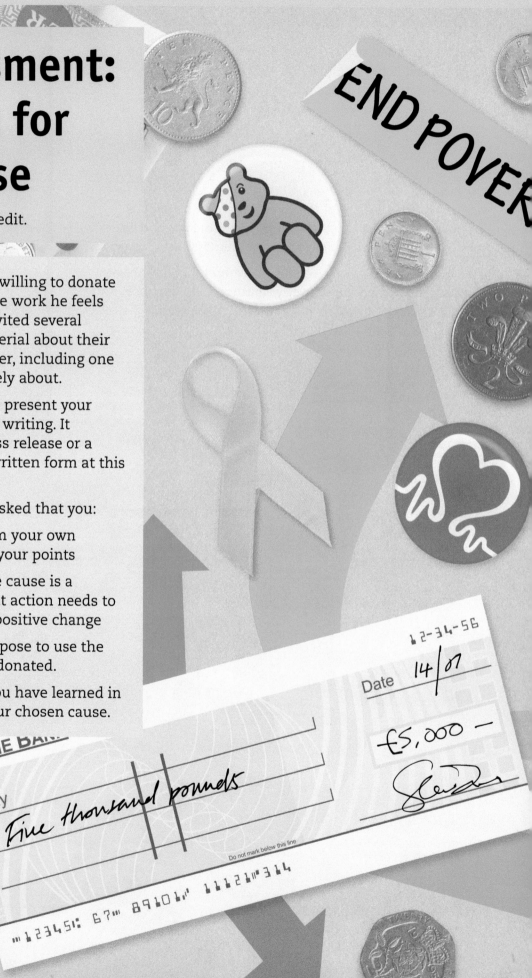

A local entrepreneur is willing to donate £5000 to a charity whose work he feels is important. He has invited several charities to submit material about their cause for him to consider, including one that you feel passionately about.

You may choose how to present your cause, as long as it is in writing. It could be a report, a press release or a persuasive speech (in written form at this stage).

The entrepreneur has asked that you:

- include findings from your own research to support your points

- clearly state why the cause is a worthy one and what action needs to be taken to make a positive change

- explain how you propose to use the money that may be donated.

Use all the skills that you have learned in this unit to promote your chosen cause.

Before you write...

Research: Make sure you have fully researched your cause, so that you have the facts and information to make your campaign accurate and informative.

Plan: Think carefully about the structure of your work, grouping your ideas into a logical sequence of paragraphs.

As you write...

Review and edit: Check that you are following your plan. Keep re-reading and saying aloud what you have written to make sure that it makes sense and will create the effects on your target audience that you want.

When you have finished writing...

Proofread: Check that your writing is accurate in terms of spelling, punctuation and grammar.

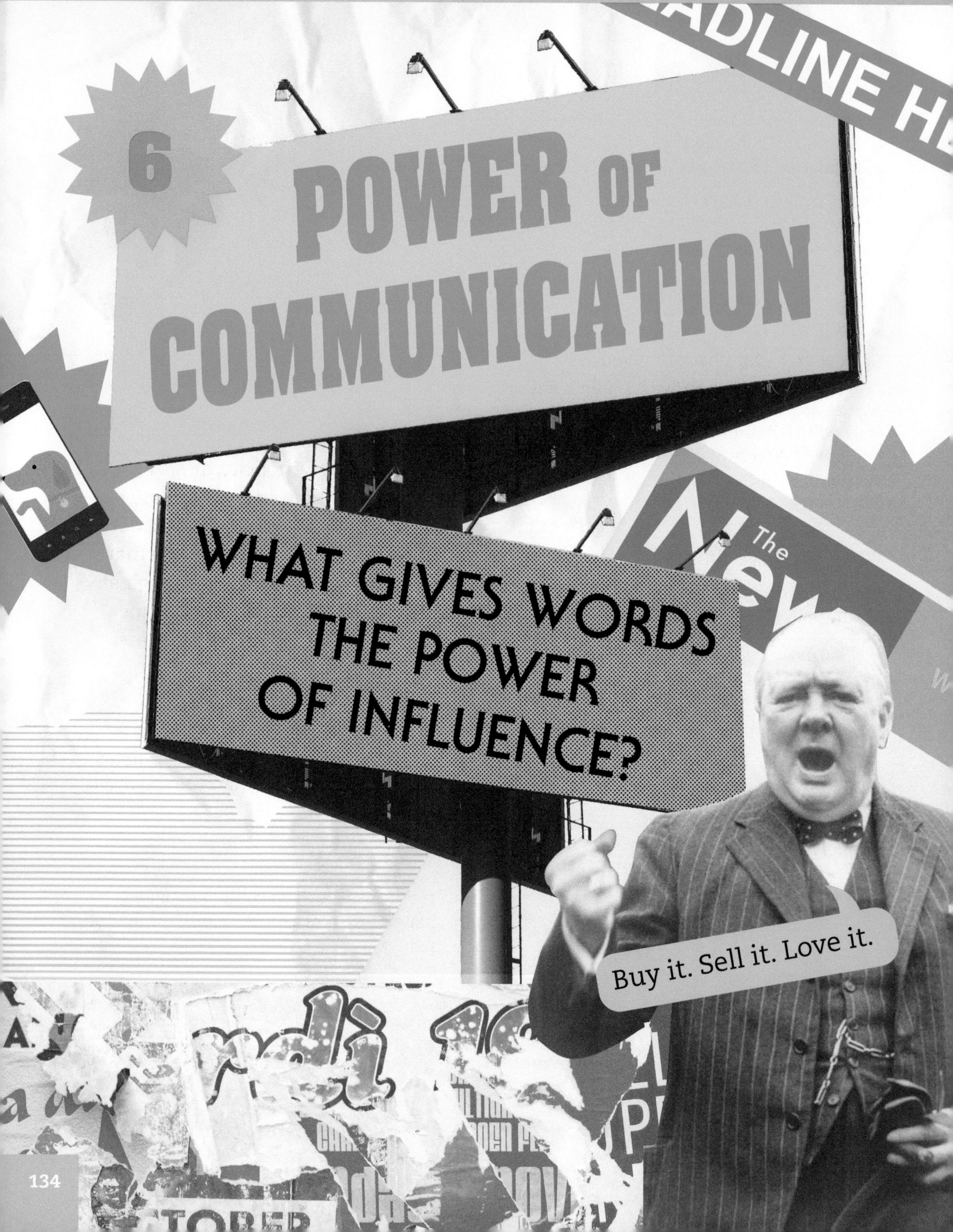

6

POWER OF COMMUNICATION

HEADLINE HE

The New

WHAT GIVES WORDS THE POWER OF INFLUENCE?

Buy it. Sell it. Love it.

Introduction

From advertisements that persuade you to buy particular products to speeches that try to change your mind, language has the power to influence what you think. People who can manipulate and control the language that they use can influence the world around them, and even change the course of history.

In this unit, you will explore the power of words and find out how writers and speakers have used language to influence others, as well as use these techniques yourself in your own speech and writing.

ignite INTERVIEW
Dominic Gettins, Head of writing for an advertising agency

There is an interesting saying that people fall in love with pictures but act on words. The words are the ideas that persuade you to take an interest in a product. What makes one advert more noticeable than another is simplicity, almost always. All the time it is very important not to think of your audience as a general mass of people but to think of them individually. Life is much more interesting if people just do something original, something that is their identity, not someone else's. The best way to create ideas is to share.

Activities

1. Discuss the advertisements you have watched or seen. Which ones do you think are the most effective and why?

2. Try to sell your pen or pencil to somebody else. Think about the ways you could persuade them that your pen or pencil is something that they need.

135

1 Every Word Counts

↻ Objective

Explore how rhetorical devices are used to create particular effects in advertising.

too good to refuse

Just too tasty

live it and love it

The language of advertising is language that is chosen to persuade. Identifying the **rhetorical devices** advertisers use and exploring the effects these create can help you to become a more critical **consumer**. One way advertisers try to influence consumers to buy particular products is through the use of advertising **slogans**.

✎ Activities

1 Match each of the advertising slogans below to the persuasive technique it uses. (Some slogans may use more than one technique.)

Slogans

Because you're worth it

Melts in your mouth, not in your hands

Leave a man, come back a hero!

Serious fuel for serious athletes

Buy it. Sell it. Love it.

8 out of 10 owners who expressed a preference said their cat prefers it.

Have a break, have a KitKat.

The mint with the hole

Persuasive techniques

Direct address: using 'you' to address the reader

Alliteration: repetition of words that begin with the same sound

Facts: statements that can be proven to be true

Opinions: something based on a belief or point of view

Repetition: repeating a word or words

Exaggeration: to show something as better than it really is

Statistics: use of percentages or a number 'out of' (e.g. 1 out of 10)

Rule of three: grouping words or phrases in threes for rhetorical effect

So soft
So smooth

2 How many of the slogans did you recognize? Can you identify the product each one is used to advertise?

3 Discuss the effects of the techniques used in each slogan on the reader. Copy and complete the grid below to record your ideas

Slogan	Technique	Effect
Because you're worth it		This implies that the company wants to give you something valuable that will make you feel special.

Support

Use phrases such as:

- This shows…
- This makes the reader think…
- This suggests…
- This emphasizes…

4 Look at the mobile phone advertisements on pages 138–139. Which advertisement do you find most persuasive? Think about the impact of the following on you as a reader:

- the product slogan
- the choice of images
- the adjectives chosen
- the persuasive techniques used.

📖 Glossary

rhetorical device writing technique used to persuade readers or listeners

consumer someone who buys or uses a product

slogan a short, memorable phrase used to describe a product or its benefits

5 Role-play a conversation where you recommend one of the phones to a friend who is looking for a new mobile. Try to use some of the persuasive techniques you have explored in the conversation.

More to explore

Works Hard
Drives Smarter

20:20 Mobile Exclusive Bundle

EXCLUSIVE 3 Months FREE
Trafficmaster Smartnav Mobile

With selected Blackberry ® smartphones from 20:20 Mobile
Avoiding queues is simple. So don't put up with them on the road. Smartnav for your BlackBerry ® smartphone knows where the traffic is and can find you the fastest way around it. But that's not the smartest part; if we can see you're better off staying where you are, we will tell you that too.

You get clear and simple turn-by-turn instructions sent to you and, if you need it, assistance from an actual person. You don't even have to know exactly where your destination is, they'll find it for you! Smartnav is different. It really is.

BlackBerry.

trafficmaster smartnav mobile

What will you bring to life?

hTC BoomSound™
Dual frontal stereo speakers

hTC BlinkFeed™
Live home screen

hTC Zoe™
Your gallery brought to life

The new
hTC one

htc.com

2 Power of Presentation

↺ Objective

Explore how choices of form, layout and presentation create persuasive effects.

Readers can be influenced by the way a text is presented as well as by what is written. Many persuasive texts, such as printed and TV advertisements, leaflets and websites, use **presentational devices** to achieve their purpose and influence their audience.

Look at the two webpages on the right. You have been asked to review them for an advertising company. The Lego webpage is the 'Create & Share' part of the Lego website. The Transformers webpage is promoting an online game, Botshots.

✎ Activities

1 Make notes on how effectively the websites use presentational devices to achieve their purpose and influence their audience. Consider:

- the purpose of each website
- the target audience of each website
- the presentational devices used and their effects.

2 Discuss how effective you think each website is in appealing to its target audience. Give each website a rating, on a scale of 1 to 5, with 5 being the highest.

ignite INTERVIEW

'Life is much more interesting if people do something original, something that is their identity, not someone else's.'

Dominic Gettins

3 Write an email to the advertising company who asked you to review the websites. Explain in your email which website you feel uses presentational devices most effectively. Give reasons for your decision.

☑ Progress Check

Think of a product you love – it might be something you eat, a video-game you've played or a gadget you use. Create a **pitch** for a website for this product. Your pitch should explain:

- what the product is
- who it is aimed at
- the presentational devices you will use in your website and why.

📖 Glossary

presentational devices things used in addition to the writing in a text, e.g. headings, subheadings, photos, illustrations, graphics, font size and style, colour, bullet points, etc.

pitch a short speech to people who will pay for the advertising to persuade them that the advertisements will get customers to spend money

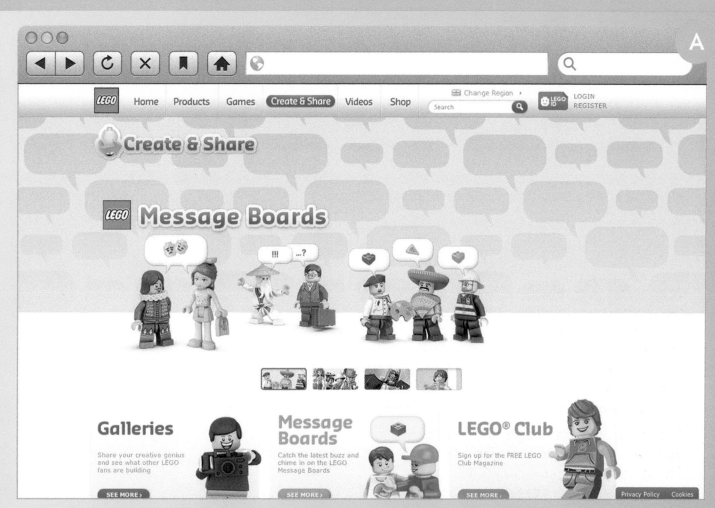

③ Emotional Appeal

↻ Objective

Develop understanding of how emotive language and other literary devices can be used to persuade.

Persuasive texts, such as charity letters, leaflets and TV advertisements, often use **emotive language** to **manipulate** a reader's or listener's feelings, e.g. by encouraging them to feel sympathy, to give money or to take action.

Now read the letter on page 143 from the animal charity Dogs Trust.

✎ Activities

1 Whose point of view is presented in the letter? Discuss how this works to help persuade the reader to support the charity. Think about:

- the **first-person pronouns** used and the effects these create

- the **anecdotes** included and the impact they have.

SPAG

2a Pick out examples of emotive language from the letter.

2b For each example, explain what emotional response is expected from the reader.

📖 Glossary

emotive language   words used to create an emotional response

manipulate   change

first-person pronoun   pronouns that refer to the writer or speaker, e.g. 'I', 'we', 'me', 'us', 'mine', 'my', 'our'

anecdote   a short account of a real incident from someone's life

rhetorical question   a question asked for effect that doesn't require an answer

3 Which of the following persuasive techniques does the letter use? For each example you find, explain how it helps to persuade the reader to support the charity.

- Direct address
- Alliteration
- Facts
- Opinions
- Repetition
- **Rhetorical questions**
- Exaggeration
- Statistics
- Rule of three

🕐 Extra Time

How does the letter try to appeal to people who love dogs? Consider the words, the images and the presentation.

Dear Mr Clark,

I was all alone and so scared. The world became such a frightening place the day I was abandoned. At first, when my owner took me out in the car, I thought we were going for a walk in the country. But then we stopped and he just pushed me out and drove off. I tried to follow him, but it was no good. What had I done to make him do a thing like that? I was part of the family. I thought we were so happy together.

Please help lonely dogs find a little love in the world.

I waited and waited for him to come back. Then it got dark and night came. I'd never been on my own before. Who was going to look after me now? I was really scared and so hungry all the time. In the end I just curled up in a ditch trying to keep warm. I don't know how long I was there, but then a man found me. He was so kind to me. I think he saved my life. It was because of him that I was brought here to Dogs Trust.

£3 a month from you means a dog like me need never be lonely again.

My name's Sammy. And I'm writing to you to tell you about Dogs Trust. They took me in, gave me a home and fed me up until I was strong again. They mended all my cuts and bruises and gave me a whole world of love and kindness. It was so different from the huge, frightening, empty world I'd been living in. I'll never forget how good it felt on that first night just to be indoors where it was so warm and cosy.

£3 a month makes the world a happier place for a dog like me.

The food, heating and medical bills all add up – Dogs Trust spends over £2 million every year just on vets bills! To give us the care we need, they depend entirely on people like you supporting them with a regular donation of £3 a month.

Thank you for reading my letter. Just £3 a month might be **the difference between life and death**. It certainly was for me. If you could find it in your heart to make a donation, your generosity really would make the world a better place for so many dogs.

Wags and licks,

Sammy

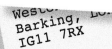

Westo... Barking, ... IG11 7RX

Benidorm

4 Building an Argument

↻ Objective

Trace the development of a writer's argument in a text.

Read the formal letter on page 145. It was sent to the *Daily Telegraph* newspaper by Jonathan Kent, the co-founder of the campaign group Leave Our Kids Alone. As you read, think about how the writer structures his argument, from presenting an opening demand to providing reasons and examples to support it.

✎ Activities

1a Re-read the first paragraph. What is the writer's viewpoint on advertising aimed at children? What does he want to happen?

↔ Stretch

Who does Kent want to take action? They are not directly mentioned in the letter.

1b In the first paragraph, which words helped you to identify the writer's viewpoint? Pick out three examples and comment on the effects of these words.

2 Look at the way the writer uses the first-person pronoun 'we' in the letter. What effect does this create? **SPAG**

3a Identify the facts and evidence the writer uses in each paragraph to support his argument.

3b Pick out emotive language he uses in each paragraph to persuade the reader.

3c Create a subheading to summarize each paragraph of the letter.

4 Does the writer end the letter with facts or emotive language? How effective do you think the ending of the letter is?

5 Discuss in pairs or small groups your views about advertising aimed at children. Refer to specific examples if you can. Do you agree or disagree with the arguments the writer of the letter opposite makes?

Letters to the Editor

Ban advertising aimed at young children

Sir – We want to see an immediate end to all advertising aimed at children of primary school age and younger. We have sleepwalked into a situation where the advertising industry, worth £12 billion a year in Britain alone, is allowed to turn techniques designed to manipulate adult emotions and desires on to children as young as two or three. This is wrong.

Almost all children under 11 depend on their parents for money. So advertising makes heavy use of 'pester power', as it is more effective than targeting parents directly. Yet a civilised society should require advertisers to sell to parents, not to children. When children are learning about the cost of material things, and about managing small quantities of money, they should be free to do so without the pressures put on them by advertising.

As things stand, we are in danger of turning out young consumers rather than young citizens – people who define themselves more by what they buy than by what they can contribute to society. Children should be free to channel their energies into forming friendships, discovering their talents and unleashing their imaginations; things that cost little but whose value is immeasurable.

Bans on advertising aimed at young children are already working in places such as Sweden, Quebec and Greece. It's time for a similar ban here.

Jonathan Kent

Co-founder, Leave Our Kids Alone

More to explore

145

Read the newspaper article on page 147. It was written by Matilda Reid, a *Daily Telegraph* journalist, in response to a call to ban advertising aimed at young children.

Activities continued

6a The writer begins by re-expressing other people's arguments. Summarize what she says in a short sentence.

6b How does the writer develop her arguments further through the remainder of the article?

6c The writer includes an anecdote about her children. Do you think this is persuasive? Give reasons for your answer.

7 Write a letter to the *Daily Telegraph* presenting your point of view on the campaign to ban adverts aimed at young children. You should:

- use an appropriately formal style, using **Standard English**

- include arguments, evidence and anecdotes to support the points you make

- structure your letter to present your argument in the most effective way.

Glossary

Standard English the variety of English that is regarded as 'correct' and is used in more formal situations. It is not specific to any geographical area and can be spoken or written.

BAN ADS AIMED AT CHILDREN?

There's no doubting that advertisers are tuned into making the most of 'pester power' – indirectly forcing parents to buy products by capturing their children's attention, knowing that their children will then nag their parents for the latest gimmick.

However, surely it's up to the parent to say 'no' to their children's demands, especially if they have requested expensive or useless products. Banning adverts is not going to stop children wanting things.

My children are four and two and they hate adverts. The second their television programme has finished, they shout out: 'It's gone', meaning their cartoon has finished, the ads have come on and they want me to do something about it. I now pre-record their shows so that I can fast-forward through the ads.

My daughter, who is four and a half, has only ever pointed out two things that have caught her attention from the television: furry animal slippers and Care Bear soft toys.

Well, no amount of 'pester power' is going to get me to buy slippers with animal's ears that pop up and down as you walk along and, from past experience, I know that a Care Bear teddy will simply end up in the basket, along with all the other discarded animals.

My son can barely sit still through a five-minute episode of Peppa Pig – so once the ads come on, he's up and off – climbing over the sofas or demanding a biscuit.

They are not exactly an advertiser's dream target market.

Rather than call for a ban on all advertising for children of primary school age and under, surely it's better to focus on developing parenting skills.

It only takes one or two birthdays and Christmases to learn that most children will cast aside the latest expensive toy in favour of the wrapping paper or a brightly-coloured ribbon.

And by the time they reach the age of nine, 10 or 11 years old, parents should have mastered the art of saying 'no', however much pester power their children muster up.

5 Debating the Issue

↻ Objective

Develop effective debating skills, using a range of techniques to present points of view persuasively.

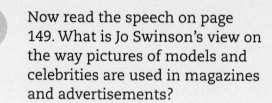

A debate is where a specific topic is discussed, with people taking it in turns to present their arguments about the topic. In a formal debate, the two opening speakers give speeches presenting their opposing arguments. After that, other people can present their arguments on both sides of the debate. A successful debater is someone who can use their persuasive skills to convince others to agree with their point of view.

✎ Activities

1. Before you read the speech on page 149, discuss the following questions.

   - What do you think about the way pictures of people your age are used in magazines and advertisements?

   - Do you think it is acceptable to **airbrush** pictures of models to make them look better?

   - Do you think the pictures of models and celebrities used in advertisements and magazines have a negative impact on how readers feel about their own bodies?

2. Now read the speech on page 149. What is Jo Swinson's view on the way pictures of models and celebrities are used in magazines and advertisements?

3. How does Jo Swinson attempt to persuade people to support her argument? Find examples of the persuasive techniques that she uses.

   For each example you have found, explain how it helps persuade listeners to agree with the argument made.

4. In what way has reading this speech changed your opinion about the issue? Debate your ideas.

📖 Glossary

airbrush   to alter a picture digitally, e.g. by making someone appear thinner

The MP Jo Swinson made the following speech in a House of Commons debate about the impact airbrushed pictures of models have on the way ordinary people feel about their bodies.

Extract from a speech by MP Jo Swinson about airbrushed pictures of models

Nowadays we cannot escape media images of impossibly beautiful people, whether on magazine covers, billboards or in newspapers. There is increasing pressure on people – especially women and girls, but increasingly men and boys – to make themselves as beautiful as possible.

Beauty itself seems no longer to be in the eye of the beholder. Instead of a wide range of body shapes and sizes being presented, we are fed a restricted diet of one narrow ideal of beauty. The cult of ultra-thin is worshipped by those aspiring to look like the skinny models on the catwalks or the teeny-tiny celebrities in the magazines. Those in the public eye who commit the ultimate sin of eating and being a normal size are named and shamed, with articles and photos documenting their fall from grace. Some people say that that has always been the case, but Marilyn Monroe would be called fat by today's standards, and even the fit and slender Cindy Crawford would look large in comparison with her size zero counterparts.

The skinny ideal is reinforced by the media. If we go into a newsagent's today, particularly in January, the magazine headlines scream out the obsession with thinness: 'My fight for a new body', 'Diet special: how we got our amazing bikini bodies' or, especially worrying, 'Diet or die!' All those are headlines in magazines that are currently on sale.

Increasingly, the images that we see are not even real, as modern technology makes it easier than ever to manipulate pictures digitally. Retouching is widespread in the modern media. Sometimes that is done to remove the odd spot or blemish, to smooth skin or add shine to hair, but in many cases the whole shape of people's bodies has been altered – waists cinched in, breasts enlarged, legs lengthened or muscles pumped up. A recent Ralph Lauren advert showed a model who had been retouched to the extent that her waist was smaller than her head.

6 A Call to Arms

↻ Objective

Explore the rhetorical and literary devices used to persuade listeners.

Great speakers and great speeches have the power to change the course of history. During the Second World War, Winston Churchill, the British Prime Minister, delivered the speech on page 151 to encourage the nation to stand strong under the threat of invasion by the German military.

✎ Activities

1 Read the speech on page 151. What is its purpose? Think about:

- what Churchill said about the country's ability to succeed
- what he wanted the country to believe.

2 Winston Churchill was praised for the honesty of his speeches. Find any words or phrases he used that show that the fight would be difficult.

3a **SPAG** Churchill repeated the phrase 'we shall…'. Why do you think he used the pronoun 'we'? What effect does it create?

3b By using 'shall', what did Churchill hope to convey?

3c Churchill also used active verbs such as 'defend' and 'fight'. What emotions do they help create for his listeners?

4 **SPAG** Look at the sentence structures Churchill used in the speech. How do they help the persuasive power of his speech? Think about:

- the length of the sentences and the rhythm the sentences give to the speech
- how punctuation is used for emphasis and to separate items in lists.

5 Write a speech persuading others to fight for a cause, e.g. a football manager's half-time talk to a losing team. Try to use the following rhetorical and literary devices:

- repetition
- active verbs
- a final call for action.

'DEFEND' 'FIGHT'

Extract from a speech by Winston Churchill during World War II

I have, myself, full confidence that if all do their duty, if nothing is neglected, and if the best arrangements are made, as they are being made, we shall prove ourselves once again able to defend our island home, to ride out the storm of war, and to outlive the menace of **tyranny**, if necessary for years, if necessary alone. At any rate, that is what we are going to try to do. That is the resolve of His Majesty's Government – every man of them. That is the will of Parliament and the nation.

The British Empire and the French Republic, linked together in their cause and in their need, will defend to the death their native soil, aiding each other like good comrades to the utmost of their strength. Even though large tracts of Europe and many old and famous States have fallen or may fall into the grip of the **Gestapo** and all the **odious apparatus** of **Nazi** rule, we shall not flag or fail. We shall go on to the end, we shall fight in France, we shall fight on the seas and oceans, we shall fight with growing confidence and growing strength in the air, we shall defend our island, whatever the cost may be.

We shall fight on the beaches, we shall fight on the landing grounds, we shall fight in the fields and in the streets, we shall fight in the hills; we shall never surrender, and even if, which I do not for a moment believe, this island or a large part of it were **subjugated** and starving, then our Empire beyond the seas, armed and guarded by the British fleet, would carry on the struggle, until, in God's good time, the **New World**, with all its power and might, steps forth to the rescue and the **liberation** of the old.

📖 Glossary

tyranny   the control of people through fear and force

Gestapo   secret police used by Nazi Germany

odious apparatus   horrible system

Nazi   German political group led by Adolf Hitler

subjugated   defeated and controlled

New World   America

liberation   freedom

🕐 Extra Time

Read more of Winston Churchill's wartime speeches to explore the techniques he used to persuade his listeners.

7 Talking About Revolution

↺ Objectives

- Understand the cultural and historical context of a literary text.

- Explore how literary and grammatical features are used for rhetorical effect.

Powerful ideas and real-life events can be explored through fiction. George Orwell's novel *Animal Farm* is an **allegory** that uses the setting of a farm to explore the events and consequences of the **Russian Revolution**. In the extract on page 153, a pig called Old Major is persuading the other farm animals to overthrow the farmer and share their produce and harvest between themselves.

✎ Activities

1 How does Old Major try to persuade the animals to rise up against the farmer?

2 Identify the persuasive devices used in the speech. Choose three examples and explain why you think they are persuasive.

3a Re-read each paragraph and write a sentence summarizing what it is about.

3b How does the writer create links between paragraphs? Look at how each new paragraph begins and explain how this contrasts or builds on the ideas in the previous paragraph.

4 Role-play a scene where the farm animals respond to Old Major's speech. Take on the roles of different farm animals that agree or disagree with Old Major. Remember to:

- use Old Major's speech as a model for your own

- draw on the persuasive devices you have explored

- include a powerful image or instruction to end your response to Old Major's speech.

☑ Progress Check

Perform your role-play to another group, asking them to pick out three things that they feel you have done well and two things that could be improved.

Extract from *Animal Farm* by George Orwell

'Now, **comrades**, what is the nature of this life of ours? Let us face it, our lives are miserable, **laborious** and short. We are born, we are given just so much food as will keep the breath in our bodies, and those of us who are capable of it are forced to work to the last atom of our strength; and the very instant that our usefulness has come to an end we are **slaughtered** with hideous cruelty. No animal in England knows the meaning of happiness and leisure after he is a year old. No animal in England is free. The life of an animal is misery and slavery: that is the plain truth [...]

'Man is the only creature that **consumes** without producing. He does not give milk, he does not lay eggs, he is too weak to pull the plough, he cannot run fast enough to catch rabbits. Yet he is the lord of the animals. [...] You cows that I see before me, how many gallons of milk have you given in the past year? And what has happened to that milk which should have been breeding up sturdy calves? Every drop of it has gone down the throats of our enemies. And you hens, how many eggs have you laid in the last year, and how many of those eggs ever hatched into chickens? [...]

'Only get rid of Man, and the produce of our labour will be our own. Almost overnight we could become rich and free. What then must we do? Why, work night and day, body and soul, for the overthrow of the human race! That is my message to you, comrades: **Rebellion**! [...]

'I have little more to say. I merely repeat, remember always your duty of **enmity** towards Man and all his ways. Whatever goes upon two legs is an enemy. Whatever goes upon four legs, or has wings, is a friend.'

📖 Glossary

allegory where fictional characters and events are used to represent real characters and events

Russian Revolution when the government was overthrown by the workers in Russia in 1917

comrades people who belong to the same group

laborious hard work

slaughtered killed

consumes eats or uses

rebellion to go against something, usually rulers

enmity hate

8 The Power of Imagery

↺ Objective

Consider the use of imagery and rhetorical devices in a speech from Shakespeare's *Henry V*.

Imagery can be used in speeches to great persuasive effect. By creating powerful and emotive images in a listener's mind, a speaker can manipulate listeners' emotions. In the speech from William Shakespeare's play *Henry V*, the king is encouraging his troops to make a last valiant attempt to win the battle by entering the castle they are besieging through a hole that has been blown in the wall.

✎ Activities

1 Read the opening line of the speech on page 155. How does Henry address his soldiers? How might this make them feel?

📖 Glossary

imagery descriptive language that creates an image in the reader's mind

metaphor describing something as something else, not meant to be taken literally, e.g. *You are a star.*

imperative verb verb that gives an instruction to do something, usually forceful and commanding words, e.g. *close* and *imitate*

2 Read the rest of the speech. Henry uses imagery and **metaphors** from the natural world to urge his men into battle. Discuss what each of the following images means and why you think Henry has used them:

- 'imitate the action of the tiger'
- 'Disguise fair nature with hard-favour'd rage'
- 'I see you stand like greyhounds in the slips, straining upon the start'.

📚 Support

Think about the qualities that the animals described possess. What does each quality suggest about the way Henry thinks his men should behave in battle?

↔ Stretch

In this speech, Henry compares the attitude needed to that of a rock being battered by a storm. Explain why he uses this metaphor.

3 How else does Henry try to inspire his men? Discuss the ways he:

SPAG

- uses **imperative verbs** to show his authority
- praises his men and refers to England to appeal to their patriotism.

Pick out examples from the speech and discuss the effects these create.

Extract from *Henry V* by William Shakespeare

Once more unto the **breach**, dear friends, once more;

Or close the wall up with our English dead.

In peace there's nothing so becomes a man

As modest stillness and **humility**:

But when the blast of war blows in our ears,

Then imitate the action of the tiger;

Stiffen the **sinews**, summon up the blood,

Disguise fair nature with hard-favour'd rage;

Then lend the eye a terrible aspect;

Let it **pry** through the **portage** of the head

Like the brass cannon; let the brow o'erwhelm it

As fearfully as doth a **galled** rock

O'erhang and jutty his confounded base,

Swill'd with the wild and wasteful ocean.

Now set the teeth and stretch the nostril wide,

Hold hard the breath and bend up every spirit

To his full height. On, on, you noblest English.

Whose blood is **fet** from fathers of war-proof!

Fathers that, like so many Alexanders,

Have in these parts from morn till even fought

And sheathed their swords for lack of argument:

Dishonour not your mothers; now attest

That those whom you call'd fathers did beget you

Be copy now to men of grosser blood,

And teach them how to war. And you, good **yeoman**,

Whose limbs were made in England, show us here

The **mettle** of your pasture; let us swear

That you are worth your breeding; which I doubt not;

For there is none of you so mean and base,

That hath not noble **lustre** in your eyes.

I see you stand like greyhounds in the slips,

Straining upon the start. The game's afoot:

Follow your spirit, and upon this charge

Cry 'God for Harry, England, and Saint George!'

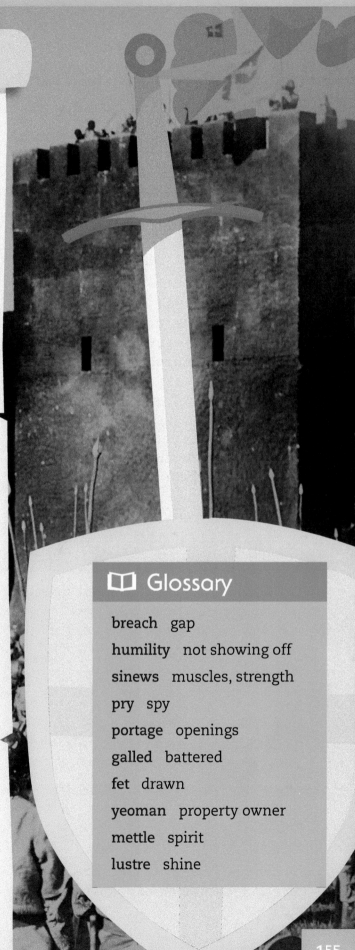

📖 Glossary

breach gap

humility not showing off

sinews muscles, strength

pry spy

portage openings

galled battered

fet drawn

yeoman property owner

mettle spirit

lustre shine

9 Assessment: Debating an Issue that Affects You

Your local council is proposing to introduce a youth curfew to cut down on vandalism and anti-social behaviour. Under the scheme, all youngsters aged 16 and under who are out on the street after 8pm will be stopped by the police and returned home immediately.

The local council has organized a public debate to hear young people's views on the proposed youth curfew scheme and you have been asked to contribute to this. You will need to:

- decide on your point of view and develop your argument

- use a range of persuasive devices to influence your audience

- use Standard English and structure your speech in an effective way.

Note that you are being tested on your spoken English skills, rather than your writing skills in this assessment.

Before you present...

Rehearse: Work in a group to discuss your views about this proposal and develop the arguments you wish to make. Look at the news report on page 157 to find out more about the effects of a similar scheme introduced in the Cornish town of Redruth. Use the knowledge and skills you have learned throughout this unit to prepare for the debate.

As you present...

Focus: Before you make your contribution to the debate, listen to the points other speakers make. When presenting your argument, try to build on what others say. Stay focused and stick to the points you wish to make.

ignite INTERVIEW

'The best way to create ideas is just to share.'

Dominic Gettins

FOR

AGAINST

This newspaper report describes the impact of a youth curfew scheme in the town of Redruth.

REDRUTH'S PIONEERING
CURFEW SLASHES CRIME
AND ANTI-SOCIAL BEHAVIOUR

REDRUTH'S pioneering night curfew has been hailed a success after police revealed anti-social behaviour had been slashed.

There had been a 60 per cent drop in anti-social behaviour.

Crime and anti-social behaviour was halved during the six-week voluntary curfew which kept under-10s off the street after 8pm and ensured under-16s were home by two hours later.

The man behind the original idea, PC Marc Griffin, said: 'From a policing point of view it's gone very well.'

At a meeting to air their views on the curfew, residents praised the success of the operation. Audrey Hambley, 68, a Close Hill resident for 36 years, said: 'It's been brilliant, really lovely. But I was dreading it ending.

'I used to be afraid to go across the lane on my own in the evening, but now I'm not. Youngsters used to be drinking, shouting or in the bushes, but the last six weeks have been lovely, really really lovely and I hope it continues.'

The community was praised by police and partner agencies for making the initiative work.

Councillor Stephen Barnes said: 'It's been a great success.

'A lot of families have had to look to each other. I think it's brought families back together.'

KS3 National Curriculum and *Ignite English* mapping: **Reading**

National Curriculum: subject content	Unit 1: It's A Mystery	Unit 2: Words of War	Unit 3: Appearance and Reality	Unit 4: Technology Matters	Unit 5: Campaign for a Cause	Unit 6: Power of Communication
Reading a wide range of fiction and non-fiction, including in particular whole books, short stories, poems and plays with a wide coverage of genres, historical periods, forms and authors. The range will include high-quality works from:	L1, L5	L3	L6	L3, L6	L3, L5, L6, L7, L8, L9	L2, L3, L4, L5, L6
• English literature, both pre-1914 and contemporary, including prose, poetry and drama	L2, L4, L7, L8, L9	L1, L2, L4, L5, L7, L8, L9, L10	L1, L2, L3, L4, L5, L9	L2		L7
• Shakespeare (two plays)			L7, L8			L8
• seminal world literature						
Choosing and reading books independently for challenge, interest and enjoyment	L1					
Re-reading books encountered earlier to increase familiarity with them and provide a basis for making comparisons						
Learning new vocabulary, relating it explicitly to known vocabulary and understanding it with the help of context and dictionaries	L1 (TC), L2 (TC), L4 (TC)		L4	L1 (TC), L2 (TC)	L4	
Making inferences and referring to evidence in the text	L2, L3, L4, L7, L9	L3, L4, L5, L7, L10	L1, L2, L5, L9			L8
Knowing the purpose, audience for and context of the writing and drawing on this knowledge to support comprehension	L1	L2, L3, L4, L5, L7, L9	L7 (TC)	L2, L3	L3, L5, L6, L7, L8, L9	L1, L2, L3, L4, L6
Checking their understanding to make sure that what they have read makes sense	L2, L3, L5, L9	L4, L5, L7, L8, L9	L1, L2, L3, L4, L7, L8		L3, L7, L9	L4, L5, L7
Knowing how language, including figurative language, vocabulary choice, grammar, text structure and organizational features, presents meaning	L2, L3, L4, L7 (TC), L8	L1, L2, L3, L4, L5, L8, L9, L10	L2, L3, L4, L7 (TC), L8, L9	L2, L3	L3, L5, L6, L7, L8, L9	L1, L2, L3, L4, L5, L6, L7, L8
Recognizing a range of poetic conventions and understanding how these have been used		L2, L4, L8 L5, L7, L9, L10	L3			L8
Studying setting, plot and characterization, and the effects of these	L2, L4, L5, L6, L7, L8, L9	L4, L5	L1, L2, L5, L8, L9	L2		
Understanding how the work of dramatists is communicated effectively through performance and how alternative staging allows for different interpretations of a play			L7, L8			L8 (TC)
Making critical comparisons across texts		L1 (TC), L5, L10			L7	L1, L2
Studying a range of authors, including at least two authors in depth each year	L2, L3, L7, L8, L9	L1, L2, L4, L5, L7, L8, L9, L10	L1, L2, L3, L4, L5, L7, L8, L9	L2		L7

Key: L = Lesson (Student Book); TC = Teacher Companion

KS3 National Curriculum and *Ignite English* mapping: **Writing**

National Curriculum: subject content	Unit 1: It's A Mystery	Unit 2: Words of War	Unit 3: Appearance and Reality	Unit 4: Technology Matters	Unit 5: Campaign for a Cause	Unit 6: Power of Communication
Writing for a wide range of purposes and audiences, including: • well-structured formal expository and narrative essays	L3	L10				
• stories, scripts, poetry and other imaginative writing	L2 (TC), L4, L5, L7, L8, L9, L10	L4 (TC), L6, L8, L9	L1 (TC), L4, L5	L6 (TC)	L4 (TC), L6 (TC), L7 (TC)	
• notes and polished scripts for talks and presentations	L4 (TC)			L6, L8	L9, L10	L5 (TC), L6
• a range of other narrative and non-narrative texts, including arguments, and personal and formal letters	L1, L3 (TC), L6 (TC)	L2 (TC), L6 (TC)	L1, L2 (TC), L5 (TC)	L4	L1, L3, L5, L6, L7, L8, L9 (TC), L10	L2, L3, L4
Summarizing and organizing material, and supporting ideas and arguments with any necessary factual detail	L3	L10	L1	L3, L5, L6	L3, L5 (TC), L9	L4
Applying their growing knowledge of vocabulary, grammar and text structure to their writing and selecting the appropriate form	L1 (TC), L4, L7 (TC), L8, L10	L3, L6, L8, L9	L5	L4, L6	L3, L5, L7, L8, L9, L10	L3, L4, L6
Drawing on knowledge of literary and rhetorical devices from their reading and listening to enhance the impact of their writing	L7, L10	L6, L8, L9			L10	L6
Considering how their writing reflects the audiences and purposes for which it was intended	L5 (TC), L6, L10			L4, L6	L8, L10	
Amending the vocabulary, grammar and structure of their writing to improve its coherence and overall effectiveness	L5 (TC), L8, L10	L6		L4, L6	L10	
Paying attention to accurate grammar, punctuation and spelling; applying the spelling patterns and rules set out in English Appendix 1 to the Key Stage 1 and 2 programmes of study for English	L10	L3, L6 (TC)		L6	L10	

Key: L = Lesson (Student Book); TC = Teacher Companion

KS3 National Curriculum and *Ignite English* mapping: **Grammar and vocabulary**

National Curriculum: subject content	Unit 1: It's A Mystery	Unit 2: Words of War	Unit 3: Appearance and Reality	Unit 4: Technology Matters	Unit 5: Campaign for a Cause	Unit 6: Power of Communication
Extending and applying the grammatical knowledge set out in English Appendix 2 to the Key Stage 1 and 2 programmes of study to analyse more challenging texts	L4, L7	L2, L3	L2		L3, L5, L6, L9	L3, L4, L6, L8
Studying the effectiveness and impact of the grammatical features of the texts they read	L4, L7	L2, L3	L2, L9		L3, L5, L6, L8, L9	L1, L3, L4, L6, L7, L8
Drawing on new vocabulary and grammatical constructions from their reading and listening, and using these consciously in their writing and speech to achieve particular effects	L4, L7			L4, L6, L9	L3, L5, L9	L3, L4, L6
Knowing and understanding the differences between spoken and written language, including differences associated with formal and informal registers, and between Standard English and other varieties of English					L3, L5 (TC)	L6
Using Standard English confidently in their own writing and speech	L1, L2	L2, L10	L9	L4, L5, L6, L9	L2, L3, L5, L7, L9, L10	L4, L6, L9
Discussing reading, writing and spoken language with precise and confident use of linguistic and literary terminology	L4, L7, L8	L2, L3, L4, L5, L7, L9	L1, L2, L3	L2	L3, L5, L6	L1, L3, L4, L6, L8

Also available: A wealth of SPAG interactives on Kerboodle LRA 1, 2 and 3.

KS3 National Curriculum and *Ignite English* mapping: **Spoken English**

National Curriculum: subject content	Unit 1: It's A Mystery	Unit 2: Words of War	Unit 3: Appearance and Reality	Unit 4: Technology Matters	Unit 5: Campaign for a Cause	Unit 6: Power of Communication
Using Standard English confidently in a range of formal and informal contexts, including classroom discussion	L1, L3 (TC)		L6, L8 (TC)	L1, L6, L7, L8 (TC)	L1, L2	L4, L5, L9
Giving short speeches and presentations, expressing their own ideas and keeping to the point	L6 (TC)		L6 (TC)	L5, L9	L8 (TC), L9	L6 (TC)
Participating in formal debates and structured discussions, summarizing and/or building on what has been said	L3 (TC)	L1 (TC)		L1, L7	L1, L2	L5 (TC), L9
Improvising, rehearsing and performing play scripts and poetry in order to generate language and discuss language use and meaning, using role and intonation, tone, volume, mood, silence, stillness and action to add impact	L2, L5	L1 (TC), L2 (TC), L4, L7	L1 (TC), L3 (TC), L4 (TC), L6, L7, L8 (TC)			L7, L8

Key: L = Lesson (Student Book); TC = Teacher Companion